Best Wishes
Dave Swint
Sharon Swint

The Story Behind the Clay

A Comprehensive Guide to Commissioned
Van Briggle Specialty Pieces

By

David O. Swint Jr.
&
Sharon Hester Swint

Cover Photo

Background Image is of 4th Street in Ramona, Colorado

Van Briggle pieces from L to R: 1914 Sigma Chi/Half Way House Mug
1920s/30s Kappa Sigma Paperweight
1914 Bruin Inn Mug

Background Photo Courtesy of Colorado Springs Pioneers Museum Starsmore Center
For Local History Colorado Springs, CO USA

Van Briggle Group Photo by David O. Swint Jr.
Compilation Image by David O. Swint Jr.

Published By:
Pikes Peak Publishing Company
1414 North Tejon Street
Colorado Springs., CO 80907
(719) 632-1743

Printed By:
Walsworth Publishing Company, Inc.
306 N. Kansas Avenue
Marceline, MO 64658

Additional copies of this book
can be purchased at:
http://www.vanbrigglebook.com
or
vanbrigglebook@aol.com

ISBN 0-9767349-0-7
Library of Congress Control Number: 2005902508

The Story Behind the Clay

Table of Contents

Introduction 4

Chapter 1 From the Beginning...6

Chapter 2 Dear Ole' Bruin Inn 32

Chapter 3 Barbecue Days at Colorado College 46

Chapter 4 Gentlemen Only..56

Chapter 5 Bars and Brass Rails 66

Chapter 6 Greeks...76

Chapter 7 Along the Cog Road 84

Chapter 8 Mission of Bells 96

Chapter 9 The Boys Back Home 102

Chapter 10 Book and Bond 108

Chapter 11 Odds and Ends 119

Color Plates...128

Price Guide 146

Works Cited 149

Index 154

Introduction

The Story Behind the Clay
A Comprehensive Guide to Commissioned Van Briggle Specialty Pieces

For several decades, David and Sharon have been avid Van Briggle Pottery collectors. She began in the 1970s with a small vase style #410 in a beautiful mulberry color. David purchased his first piece in the town of Victor, Colorado one summer in an old antique store. From the beginning, their pieces were more than lovely. They each had a history. In the case of David's first piece, in mountain crag brown, which was the glaze formula lost in the flood of 1935, there were always questions. One could date them by style, color and markings but what after that? What was their background? Who purchased them and in what home had they resided? Did some tourist pick one up while visiting Colorado or did an art aficionado select the piece for its form and glaze?

By accident, and partly because of a shortage of money, they gathered pieces from time to time, but not a Lorelei, Three Graces or a lovely lamp but a more utilitarian piece – a tumbler, or a mug. Sometimes these pieces had inscriptions on them, sometimes a person's name. Slowly it became apparent that with these Van Briggle pieces, there were clues to their history. Each piece that had been found had a story to tell and that is how they began. They were part collectors, part historians and part detectives. Their hope is that you find the story behind these pieces they have selected as interesting as they do, and that you, like them, will see more than pretty pieces of clay. They are indeed a reflection of their place in history and in the world.

Acknowledgements

Along the way many interesting people have helped unravel the story behind the clay. Our heartfelt thanks go out to: Leah Davis Witherow, Jessy Randall, Ginny Kiefer, Dave Ryan, Katie Gardner, Frank Frazier, Mike Doty, Bill Abbott, Kelly Murphy, Darlynn Mangus, Craig Stevenson, Miles Schmidt, Todd & Kathleen Sutherland, Richard Sasicki, Josie Fania, Bob Teas and Kathy Honea, Andrew Wolf, William R. Massa Jr., Cathy Wright, Susan Conley, Mary Davis, The Colorado Springs Pioneers Museum, Special Collections of the Colorado College Tutt Library, The Pikes Peak Library District, Yale University Library, Chris and Cindy Williams, Evelyn Dyson, and Katherine Scott Sturdevant for her editorial assistance.

Dedication

This book is lovingly dedicated to our spouses and children who, from the beginning, supported the idea of our writing a book. Little did they know the project would go on for several years. David's wife, Teresa, and daughter, Emily, as well as Sharon's husband, David Sr., and other sons, Bill, Kris, and daughter, Sarah, put up with our endless hours in front of the computer writing and rewriting. They endured the long days of museum and library research, missed meals, and times when we just couldn't "be disturbed." Thanks to all of you for helping make *The Story Behind the Clay* a reality and for loving us all the way.

Lastly, it should be noted that David and Sharon found that the joy surrounding this project was truly in the search, and particularly in working together.

Chapter 1

From the Beginning

Other authors have told the Van Briggle story time and time again with little new information surfacing, until now. Most books have concentrated on the historical aspects of the pottery along with the standard pottery line. This book focuses on the historical facet of the pottery but ties it to items produced for businesses, special occasions, colleges, fraternal organizations, and the like during the Twentieth Century and particularly the early 1900s. It also shows how the Van Briggle Pottery influenced the shaping of Colorado Springs through its interaction with the community.

Artus Van Briggle was born in Felicity, Ohio, on March 21ˢᵗ, 1869. He was the son of Eugene Van Briggle (originally Van Brueghel), of Flemish descent, and Martha Bryan of Kentucky. From an early age it was evident that Artus would follow his family's legacy by becoming an artist. At the age of seventeen, Artus moved to Cincinnati to study pottery. As an apprentice, under Karl Langenbeck of the Avon Pottery, Artus gained the necessary skills to take his talent to the next step. In addition, he attended the Cincinnati Art School, the School of Design at the Mechanics Institute, and began working at the renowned Rookwood Pottery as a decorator.

In 1893, Rookwood sent Artus Van Briggle to Europe to study at the Académie Julian and eventually the Beaux Arts Academy, further honing his skills as a world-class artist. There he won several awards for his paintings and drawings. While in France, Artus began to visit the Louvre, Musee des Arts Decoratifs, and other fine museums discovering the ceramic ware from the Fourteenth Century Ming Dynasty. His fascination with the "dead" glazes was evident.

> *As a result of much examination and thought, he reached the conclusion that in principle the modern highly vitrified and bright glazes were inartistic and that, through experiment, a partial return at least might be made to the soft dull surfaces of early Oriental fictiles, to reproduce which would be to restore a lost art.* (Sargent 418)

During Artus's sabbatical, he met an American woman, also studying in Europe, and they began to keep company. In 1895, Artus Van Briggle and Anne Lawrence Gregory became engaged. Not long after their engagement, Anne returned to Pennsylvania and Artus to Cincinnati to continue his work at Rookwood. Following his return, Artus began experimenting with matte glazes in a small kiln that Maria Storer (founder of the Rookwood Pottery) gave him. With few successes, it took two years for Artus to somewhat perfect the glaze. He exhibited his achievement on a piece designed specifically for Mrs. Storer; an early version of Artus's most famous creation - the

Lorelei vase. Mrs. Storer was delighted and encouraged Artus to continue his experiments both in glaze development and designs in low relief. Inspired, Artus continued his experiments for Mrs. Storer and Rookwood.

In 1899, however, Artus began to feel the effects of tuberculosis – a disease he had contracted a few years earlier. The debilitating effects of this disease forced him to sever his long relationship with Rookwood. This created hard feelings with managers and co-workers after investing so much in his education. In a sign of good faith and fearing the secrets of the dead glaze would be lost again, he handed over to Rookwood the glaze formulas with the understanding that they would only be used in the event of his death. Following the death of Artus Van Briggle, Rookwood began to incorporate the matte glaze into their regular pottery line, however Albert Valentine, a senior Rookwood decorator, never gave credit to Artus for discovering the lost glaze.

Artus Van Briggle arrived in Colorado Springs, by train, in March 1899. Commonly referred to as a "lunger," Artus moved to the Springs in the hopes of improving his health in the dry western air. He immediately found residence in the home of Asaheal Sutton, cousin to his long time friend Billy Sutton. Later that year he moved to a boarding house at 501 N. Tejon and met Professor William Strieby, a chemistry professor at Colorado College. Dr. Strieby provided Artus with laboratory space and a small kiln to conduct experiments with local clays and on new glazes. *"It was a crudely built kiln made of common ordinary brick with a shell of fireproof lining, and having only a natural draft.* (Bogue 15) This is where he achieved his first real successes, and in 1901 he believed he had perfected the matte glaze. He applied the new glaze to a six-inch vase done in low relief similar to the 1898 piece designed for Mrs. Storer. It was an ivory peach color. Artus sent several of the prior test pieces he had fired in Dr. Strieby's kiln to Mrs. Storer for review. She was so taken by the beauty of the glazes and designs that she sought advice from some of Europe's premier judges of art and she included the pieces in the Rookwood display at the 1899 Paris Exposition. Both the judges and salon participants marveled at Artus' pieces. Mrs. Storer wrote, *"it was the most admired of all the ware in the Rookwood exhibit. Critics of all countries, who had found the beautiful Grueby ware of Boston too 'see,' pointed especially to the texture and touch of the Van Briggle glaze and to its exquisite semi-transparency, wherein lies what is probably its chief charm."* (Colorado Springs *Gazette*, pg. 10, Aug. 25ᵗʰ 1901)

In the summer of 1900, Anne Gregory moved to Colorado Springs and began work as the art supervisor at the Colorado Springs High School. Her close friend Alice Shinn had urged her to interview for the job. *"She was so lovely in appearance, so convincing when questioned about her preparation for the position, I felt sure she would be appointed and she was. I am sure no Art teaching in a high school ever equaled the two years she gave her pupils. The results showed it and they adored her."*

(Shinn 1) During her off time, Anne began to help Artus with his new endeavor. With

(Photo of Original Van Briggle Pottery Plant, Courtesy of The Pikes Peak Library District & Stewarts

Commercial Photographers)

the financial help of Mrs. Storer, Artus and Anne built a modest pottery studio in the back yard of Artus's cottage located at 617 N. Nevada Avenue. The studio consisted of a thrower's wheel, blunger, sifter, clay press, and a three-foot round gas-fired, down-draft kiln. The small kiln proved to be inadequate due to the unpredictability of pressured gas and was later replaced with a larger brick kiln fired by crude oil and compressed air. The studio, which eventually became the first Van Briggle Pottery, was staffed by a skilled thrower, Harry Bangs, and a young apprentice. Life was extremely taxing on both Artus and Anne, requiring them to stay up nights to monitor the kilns when firing pottery. *"The history of the founding of the Van Briggle Pottery against the odds of poor health, insufficient money, and untrained helpers is well known, but only a few intimate friends knew how almost overwhelming the struggle."* (Shinn 1) At times Artus had bed-ridden spells due to exhaustion and complications from tuberculosis. Through hard work and a passion for art, Artus and Anne persevered in their business and personal relationship, and on July 28th, 1901, they officially announced their engagement to be married.

During 1901, the glazes were greatly improved, so on the 19th of August, Artus invited several friends to the pottery to impress their initials in pieces. He then fired the pieces and gave them to the individuals as gifts. One prominent guest was the famed western artist Charles Craig. Prior to Christmas in 1901, Artus and Anne hosted a reception with a large kiln of some 200 – 300 pieces of pottery drawn. After the gathering, the townspeople attending purchased nearly every piece made from the first kiln, officially launching the Van Briggle Pottery. A newspaper article best describes the events of that day:

> Mr. A. VanBriggle, who has lately established a pottery here, gave his first reception yesterday at 617 North Nevada, where a large collection of the beautiful vases was set out for the admiration of those who thronged the rooms. The collection included practically all of the ware which has been fired since the new kiln was first started some weeks ago, and the unqualified success of the process was eloquently testified to by the ware itself, which for exquisiteness of outline, contour and color effects, and for skill in modeling has probably never before been equaled in the ceramic world. This was the verdict reached by the artists and connoisseurs who were numbered yesterday among Mr. VanBriggle's guests.
>
> The reception lasted from 9 until 5, during which crowds of people attended, and the utmost enthusiasm prevailed during the entire day. Many of the pieces were sold, but they will be left until Sunday, and these, together with the others, will be on exhibition today, and the general public is invited. In about a week an exhibit is to be made up and sent to Paris,

another to Madrid, and one will go to New York where considerable interest has been taken in the work.

Among those present yesterday were: Mr. and Mrs. Charles Craig, Mr. and Mrs. Skelton, Mr. and Mrs. Soutter, Mrs. Lawrence, Mr. and Mrs. Ormes, Mrs. Robinson, Mrs. Elizabeth Martin, Mr. W. N. Burgess, Mr. Francis Pastorius, Mr. Horace Pastorius, Mrs. F. W. Goddard, Mr. and Mrs. Sidford F. Hamp, Miss Bemis, Dr. Peavey, Mr. and Mrs. Percy Hagerman, Mr. Bert Hagerman, Mr. and Mrs. Henry Russell Wray, Miss Loomis, Professor and Mrs. Strieby, Mr. and Mrs. James C. Conner, Dr. and Mrs. Solenberger, Mrs. Abett, Miss M. Warner, Miss Bessie French, Dr. Hayden, Mr. and Mrs. D Alton Thomas, Irving Howbert, Mrs. Ahlers, Dr. and Mrs. Shett, Mr. and Mrs. Charles E. Noble, T. Maclaren, Mr. and Mrs. McClurg, Mr. Lotave, Mr. Frank Perkins, Mr. D. C. Whittlesey, Mrs. Thompson, Mr. and Mrs. A. Sutton, Mr. George D. Galloway, Mr. Hayes, Mr. R. Chisholm, Mrs. Ehrich, Miss Ehrich, Mrs. Waterman, Dr. and Mrs. Solly, Judge and Mrs. Simpson and Mrs. Taylor, Miss Crosby, Mr. and Mrs. Chester A. Arthur, Mr. Eustis, Mr. Every, Dr. Joseph Nichols, Mrs. Boas, Mrs. Bartow, Mr. and Mrs. Noyes, Professor Parsons, Mr. Phillip B. Stewart, Mr. J. McK. Ferriday, Mr. Howard

Gallop, Miss Anne Gregory, Major Remick, Mr. and Mrs. John Shields, Mr. and Mrs. Kissell, Mr. and Mrs. Peck, Dr. and Mrs. Swan and Miss Swan, Mrs. Dorsey, Mrs. Brown, Mrs. Hodgins, Miss Ridgeway, Mrs. D. V. Donaldson, Mrs. Allen, Miss Foster Dickman, George Rex Buckman, Mrs. Lunt, Mr. and Mrs. S. W. Townsend, Mrs. Lawson Sumner, Prof. E. S. Parsons. (Colorado Springs *Gazette*, pg. 5 col. 1-2, Dec. 7th 1901)

Artus obviously moved by the success of the reception stated,

How little I thought, when I was exiled to Colorado that I would everywhere here meet with so much kindness and aid! How little I expected to find in Colorado Springs the incentive to resume my work which everyone has held out to me. I feel confident of success, and I hope the city may feel my gratitude. After I am settled here I shall be more than glad to open my place to the public on Mondays and Thursdays. The kindly criticism which has already been given my ware has pleased and encouraged me more than I can say. (Artus Van Briggle 1901)

The year 1902 brought about much change at the pottery. In March a stock company was formed to generate much needed cash for improvements and staff. Stockholders included the wealthy and elite such as General William J. Palmer (founder of Colorado Springs), Mrs. Maria Storer, Clarence P. Dodge, C. Sharpless

Pastorius, T.J. Fisher, Henry Russell Wray, Asaheal Sutton, Dr. William H. Strieby, W.S. Stratton and C.M. MacNeill. With the influx of money, Artus increased the work force and added two small gas kilns in addition to the large kiln. Trained workmen were almost impossible to find, requiring Artus to teach his men everything. However, through diligent efforts he and Anne managed to move forward and, on June 12th 1902, held a private marriage ceremony at Helen Hunt's Garden near Adams Ranch on Cheyenne Mountain. Reverend Manly D. Ormes presided over the union that was attended by several close friends of the Van Briggles. Shortly after their marriage, Anne gave up her position as supervisor of art and began working at the pottery full time.

Stresses associated with the new business began to take their toll on Artus and he finally came to grips with the seriousness of his illness. Deteriorating health forced he and Anne to go to Tucson, Arizona for the winter of 1902 – 1903. George B. Young served as the young pottery's manager. Prior to their departure a young rising star joined the pottery: Frank Riddle, a gentleman with an artistic nature who was a former student of Anne's. Frank caught on quickly and began to get heavily involved with the development of glazes and eventually was credited with many of the glazes created by the pottery. Artus commented in a letter, while in Tucson: *"Pastorius wrote a hasty note yesterday in which he says your olive trial is a great success...Miss Shinn wrote us she liked the new yellow better than the old. I hope I shall, as the savings in dollars is quite worth while."* (Artus Van Briggle, Mar. 2ⁿᵈ 1904) Ambrose Schlegel was another important hire. A master potter of German descent, he came to America at age 20 in search of a new life. At age 46 he joined the pottery and was the primary thrower for Artus and Anne. Both Riddle and Schlegel became key players that shaped the early years of the new pottery.

In 1902 the pottery held an exhibition in Colorado Springs and later that same year sent twenty-four pieces to the 1903 Paris Salon. All were accepted, an unbelievable feat in that day due to the stringent criteria for entrance, especially from an American artist. Of the pieces entered, several received medals, and many of Europe's finest judges declared the pieces *"a supreme discovery in modern ceramics"* *"and it is the consensus of opinion among connoisseurs that the technical knowledge displayed is superior to that of France."* This began a pattern of numerous accolades that came to the gifted artist and his wife. Through 1903, they developed many glazes, with numerous trial pieces, and gained increased company recognition. Meanwhile Artus's frail health forced the Van Briggles to relocate to Tucson for the winter. The arid environment did little to improve his condition and his displeasure with staying there was evident in a letter to Frank Riddle. *"Mrs. Van Briggle accuses me of being homesick, but herself expresses that it will seem very nice indeed to get back there..."* (Artus Van Briggle, Mar. 2ⁿᵈ 1904)

In March of 1904, and after winning numerous honors at the 1903 Paris Salon, the Van Briggle exhibit returned to Colorado Springs to prepare for entrance into the 1904 St. Louis Louisiana Purchase Exposition, along with several new pieces to make up a display of approximately one-hundred pieces of fine pottery. Growing fame and a sense of hometown pride motivated the residents of Colorado Springs to put up the money for an exhibit pergola. Again, the pottery received much admiration and many awards, however, during the exposition Artus's health finally failed and he died at age 35 on the 4th of July, 1904. The art world was devastated and the

(Van Briggle Pergola at the 1904 St. Louis Exposition, Van Briggle Pottery Advertising Catalog, Circa 1907, Author's Collection)

exhibit in St. Louis was draped in mourning marking the loss. The night Artus Van Briggle died, Anne, along with Harry Bangs and Frank Riddle, made a death mask of the artist that is now housed at the Pioneers Museum in Colorado Springs. Artus Van Briggle was buried in Evergreen Cemetery, also located in Colorado Springs, in a private ceremony attended only by Anne, his mother, and sister Leona. An article written in the Colorado Springs *Gazette* prior to his death sums up his life: *"Of this success, purchased at the sacrifice of the most valuable human possessions – energy, time, talent and perseverance – it is not necessary to dwell. Suffice it to say that his whole life work has been devoted to the development of his one aim, and its success and recognition are his reward."* (Colorado Springs *Gazette*, pg. 15 col. 2, Jan. 1ˢᵗ 1904) Artus Van Briggle designed over three hundred pieces of pottery, himself carving all the originals by hand and many out of wax.

Following the death of her beloved husband, Anne, overcome with grief and dedicated to her husband's legacy and passion, took control and began to run the business. Later that year, the board of directors reorganized the company and changed the name to the Van Briggle Company with Anne Van Briggle as the president. Additionally, Frank Riddle left the company in 1904 and moved to Ohio where he attended Ohio State University majoring in Ceramic Engineering. Under Anne's guidance, the company evolved; new glazes and designs, commemorative items, experimentation with glazed tile and terra cotta, and an increased work staff all added to the perpetuation of an artist's dream. The pottery continued to win high praise and awards with exhibits at the 1905 Lewis and Clark Exposition in Portland, Oregon and the 1906 Boston Arts and Crafts Society's 10th Anniversary. During the Boston exhibit, Anne Van Briggle received a degree of master from the Arts and Crafts Society of Boston propelling her into a world-class artist like her late husband.

Partly through necessity but primarily because of love, Anne solicited help from prominent Colorado Springs residents and businesses to build a memorial to Artus signifying his accomplishments to the city and the world. Through the help of several businesses and townspeople, specifically General Palmer, her dream became a reality. General Palmer supplied Anne with a prime piece of real estate on the north end of Monument Valley Park along the banks of Fountain Creek. A notable local architect Nicholas Van den Arend designed a building that was pleasing to the eye and accentuated the form, color, and design specifically found within the Van Briggle ware.

The architect, Mr. N. Van den Arend, prepared plans worthy of his high reputation in both Europe and America. The result is a striking piece of architecture showing the artistic uses of gables and bringing out many features of modern decoration in polychrome tile terra cotta work. The kiln tops, spaces between windows and other vantage points are used to

display effective color treatments. In the interior, the mantel pieces are fine specimens of Van Briggle relief work. Tiles and smaller terra cotta ornamental pieces will form about one-half of the company's output.
(Glass and Pottery World, pg. 15-16, April 1908)

Construction started in 1907, with Anne designing the glazed tiles and terra cotta pieces, with the help of Emma Kinkead a young artist who had once been a student of hers. The pieces were made at the North Nevada plant with the new memorial pottery opening in September, 1908. The pottery housed some of the most modern equipment: *"The plant is equipped with a complete outfit of the latest clay-working machinery, all of which is driven by electricity."* (Colorado Springs *Gazette*, pg. 7 col. 1-7, December 3rd 1908) The newly designed coal-fired kilns allowed for a more efficient firing of pottery. The design utilized two brick walls, an inner and outer, allowing the fire to burn between the walls and never touching the pottery, enabling a well-organized use of space by eliminating the need for saggars. All this for a mere $50,000 in 1908. The new pottery was spectacular and brought together modern and architectural art all in one setting. *"Colorado Springs architect Elizabeth Wright-Ingraham, granddaughter of Frank Lloyd Wright, has noted, 'It was said that Van Den Arend and Van Briggle envisioned the use of tile in buildings all over the city and wanted to make Colorado Springs a colorful and beautiful place.' To a large extent they succeeded."* (Knauf 16)

Anne, took on the monumental endeavor to expand the pottery, by increasing the pottery staff, marketing the new ware and managing the debt, while continuing to work as an artist; an unbelievable task for a grieving single woman in the early twentieth century. Fortunately, Anne put together a team of professionals as deeply devoted to the new pottery as she was. Lyle E. Dix, with his reputation as a staunch business manager, was responsible for marketing the products, while Anne enticed Frank Riddle to come back from Ohio as an engineer supervising the construction and installation of the new equipment. He eventually became the pottery superintendent in 1908. Ambrose Schlegel continued as the head potter for the company and Anne Van Briggle was in charge of the art department. With the opening of the new pottery, the company expanded into a variety of ceramic activities; art pottery, plain glazed tile, architectural terra cotta, decorated tile, semi-vitreous tile, enameled brick chimney tops, roof tile, interior décor walls, wall fountains, decorative electrical fixtures, advertising novelties, garden pottery and furniture, lamp bases and even fireplace mantels. Anne was balancing her work with a new relationship. Etienne A. Ritter, a well respected Swiss French mining engineer with a sterling character, asked Anne to marry. On July 14th 1908 they wed.

The new pottery was the prize of the city, enabling Colorado Springs to become a world-renowned art center comparable with the great art centers of the East. The pottery's formal opening on December 3rd, 1908, included a special kiln drawn to celebrate the formal opening and upcoming Christmas season; five hundred guests attended. Finally the pottery seemed to be on track, life was good, it had achieved fame and name recognition, and the days of financial hardship were over. The company's production drastically increased both in the standard art pottery line and in specialty items. Fireplace mantles appeared in several buildings and homes throughout the city. The long time affiliation with Colorado College continued with many specialty items produced for the school. The pottery also created ornate tiles and electrical items.

Through changing times, mismanagement, or something unknown, the company started having financial problems by 1910. Frank Riddle decided to marry Miss Florence Perkins on August 9th 1910 and take a new job back east as a ceramic engineer with the American Sewer Pipe Company. The pottery reorganized as the Van Briggle Pottery and Tile Company in an attempt to relieve debt. Anne, distraught over the financial problems associated with the struggling pottery and pressured by her husband to break away and move to Denver, eventually leased the company to Edmund Deforest Curtis sometime between 1910 and 1912. *"How we longed to banish the continued anxiety of this financial struggle that was so wearing on Mrs. Van Briggle...A few years more of work in the Pottery and it passed into other hands."* (Shinn 1) Curtis, a well-educated man with a background in metallurgy, attempted to do what Anne and others couldn't; keep the pottery solvent. In 1913, however, the pottery finally closed. The bankrupt pottery was sold at auction July 29th 1913, on the east steps of the El Paso County Courthouse (now the Colorado Springs Pioneers Museum) to H. G. Lunt and George Krause, for $63,000. Lunt and Krause were unable to keep the pottery running and sold the business back to Curtis in September 1913 for the sum of $25,000.

With only a handful of people, Curtis attempted to pick up where he had left off. He achieved this in two ways: reducing costs and practically selling his soul. Realizing production costs were too high; he introduced mine tailings, from Cripple Creek gold mines, into the clay mixtures. This benefited in two ways: it reduced the clay costs by fifty percent while reportedly increasing the number of perfect pieces fired in the kilns. His determination to see the business rebound is shown in the large number of specialty items, from 1914, made for businesses in and around the city, and from the manner he marketed the pottery's products in the company's advertising catalog. It appears that his marketing promoted any ceramic related project regardless of size, shape, color, or quantity.

E. de F. Curtis .

(Signature of Edmund Deforest Curtis, Author's Collection)

"If you will write us a brief description of the kind of Pottery you desire; the size, shape (whether bowl or vase) and color, and will enclose $1.00 to cover express or postage, we

will forward the Pottery for your approval. If it is satisfactory, we will send you a bill for it, giving you credit for the $1.00 received. If you do not like it, send it back to us collect, and we will pay return charges." (Van Briggle Advertising Catalog, Circa 1914) Still with all that he did, it wasn't enough and he sold the, still fragile pottery company, to Charles B. Lansing in 1915.

Lansing was an exceptional businessman with a thick pocket book. During his tenure, he increased production, marketing, and the employment numbers. At one point he had sixteen traveling salesmen selling the company's products. He was so successful in the revitalization of the pottery that he felt comfortable enough to take a leave of absence and fight in World War I. After returning from the war in 1918, Lansing resumed his duties as head of the pottery and was also elected president of the Colorado Springs Chamber of Commerce. Continuing the sale of specialty items, the company produced items for Colorado College and the Reserve Watch, a hometown militia made up of individuals not able to fight in the war. Following Lansing's return a fire broke out, on June 25th, 1919, in the central part of the memorial pottery building causing an estimated $50,000 worth of damage. The pottery did not shut down and operated even during the rebuilding process.

The center wing of the plant was destroyed by fire last June. The fire did not stop the manufacture, however, and the building was rebuilt as quickly as possible. Some of the soft clay ware which had been placed in the kilns

was found to be fully fired when the kiln was opened. The building was

rebuilt along the same lines as the old, so that its traditional appearance

was not lost. (Colorado Springs *Gazette*, pg. 1 col. 3, April 20th 1920)

With the minor setback, Lansing continued the operation of the plant but eventually

sold the pottery in a private deal on April 19th, 1920, to I. F. Lewis.

I. F. Lewis, of Springfield, Missouri, purchased controlling interest in the Van

Briggle Art Pottery and eventually brought his brother, J. H. Lewis, into the business.

The Lewis brothers managed the company well, however, in the process they virtually

eliminated all artistic aspects of the pottery by turning it into a strictly-for-profit venture.

One exception was the Van Briggle School of Design. It trained young artists to

produce new and artistic pieces suited to the times. Aside from this, the Lewis brothers

destroyed virtually everything unique to the ware with emphasis no longer on artistic

value, but more on the bottom line. Glazes diminished to a handful of colors, and the

pottery modified original designs produced by Artus and Anne to meet a more modern

appeal for the public, effectively destroying the original artistic intent. Although Artus

Van Briggle despised them, gloss or volcanic glazes became a new cost-cutting measure.

Through the 1920s and thirties, the Lewis brothers did still produce some specialty

items, though not to the level and artistic measure of early pieces. With all that said, the

Van Briggle School of Design afforded artists such as Gene Hopkins, William Higman, Nellie Walker, O. F. Bruce, (a deaf mute who turned out originals), Fred Wills, and Clem Hull, among others, a means to design a variety of contemporary figural and standard art pottery pieces.

No longer affiliated with the pottery, Anne had lived a comfortable life in Denver Colorado since 1921, finishing her days as an impressionistic style painter of Colorado landscapes. *"Her days were never too full for creative expression along artistic lines. She had been taught to "make haste slowly in Art" and this tranquility in study was in all she undertook. Taste and talent were in her work."* (Shinn 1). It was her first love and she eventually returned to it exhibiting her paintings often under the name Anne Gregory Ritter. At the age of 61, on November 15th, 1929, Anne Van Briggle Ritter died. Her close friend Alice Shinn had this to say about her in a letter: *"To her friends she was 'steel true, blade straight,' they could count on her quiet understanding and on her helpfulness. She knew that 'Life was not a goblet to be drained but a measure to be filled,' and that was the life she lived. I am only one of many mourning today yet rejoicing in having known and loved so rare, so steadfast, so beautiful a character."* (Shinn 1)

After a brief closure during World War II, the pottery experienced a new lease on life. It updated older glazes, introduced new glazes, marketed new designs, and established the use of gloss glazes. Pieces fired with the new gloss glazes were marked "Anna Van Briggle" on the bottoms versus the traditional conjoined A and usual script writing.

> *Pieces bearing the high-gloss brown, black or blue-green glaze were introduced at Van Briggle in 1955, and until 1968 these pieces were inscribed "Anna Van Briggle" on the bottoms. From 1968 hence, the pieces read the same as the matte glaze pieces, and contain the double-A trademark. (This glaze was named in honor of Mrs. Van Briggle when it was introduced).* (Information Paper Published by the Van Briggle Pottery Company, July 1972)

In addition to the gloss glazes previously discussed there was one special gloss glaze that was produced for only three months in 1956. Commonly known as the Gold Ore Glaze; *"...a different type of pottery is made and into the glaze of some of it is incorporated powdered gold ore from Cripple Creek mines. An auriferous speckled effect is produced that is much esteemed. It is something new and has a great appeal."*
(Colorado Springs *Gazette Telegraph*, pg. 2 col. 5-7, May 20th 1956)

Two more major events happened during the 1950s: I. F. Lewis sold his interests in the pottery and moved to Phoenix leaving J. H. to run all operations. Meanwhile, concerns about a new interstate passing through the location of the memorial pottery gave J. H. serious concerns resulting in the purchase of the old Midland Railroad

Roundhouse in Colorado Springs. The pottery transformed the roundhouse into a working pottery and allowed Lewis two locations to market the Van Briggle ware. The roundhouse originally only produced gloss glaze pieces until the consolidation of all operations in 1968.

Despite concerns about the new interstate, it never did pass through the property on which the memorial pottery was located, instead passing just west of the pottery building. Even so, Lewis chose to sell the memorial pottery building to Colorado College in 1968. With the sale, all operations of the company moved to the Midland Railroad Roundhouse and the long-produced Persian Rose glaze was discontinued. Reports conflict as to why the glaze was discontinued. Two explanations were that the new gas-fired kilns in the Midland facility could not replicate the exact color or it lost its appeal with the general public.

J. H. Lewis had had enough. In 1969, Kenneth W. Stevenson became the principle owner of the Van Briggle Pottery. Starting as a bookkeeper, Stevenson learned the business, which eventually propelled him into ownership. He along with his wife, Bertha, and two sons, Craig and Jeff, carried on the Van Briggle tradition.

Partly as favors and partly as business propositions, the company began producing specialty items between the 1970s and the mid-1980s, with Craig Stevenson designing many of them. However, due to the low quantities produced per specialty item it became cost prohibitive to continue designing and selling the items. One exception was a large project the City of Colorado Springs proposed to the pottery in the early 1990s. The city proposed building a World Arena for sporting events on the south side of the city. A plan to help finance the arena while building community pride developed, which called for the design and incorporation of four Van Briggle specialty tiles into the facility. For a donation, anyone could have a tile made in someone's honor, that would be permanently affixed to the interior walls of the arena. The effort met with great success and helped meet the financial shortfalls for the Colorado Springs World Arena.

Following Stevenson's death on November 9th 1990, his wife and son Craig began to steer the company into a more traditional direction. *"During the past 50 years, a lot of stuff was made that was antithetical to Van Briggle's aesthetics, he says. He has pruned many designs from the catalogs. And he gradually is introducing his own new designs, which he says move forward but stay true to our roots."* (Arnest pg. 7 col. 4) Craig, a talented sculptor, took charge of designing new original pieces, done in low relief, consistent with the Van Briggle or Art Nouveau style. He developed new matte glazes, re-introduced old original designs and tiles, specialty items again linked the community, and the pottery began to appear around the city in architectural structures. A definitive attempt to follow the dreams of Artus and Anne Van Briggle relating to texture, color, love of the craft, and perfection are evident at the Van Briggle Pottery today.

(Photo of Van Briggle Memorial Pottery Building Circa 1910, Author's Collection)

1914 Bruin Inn Mug
(Author's Collection)

Chapter 2

Dear Ole' Bruin Inn

In 1882, Colorado College President E. P. Tenney created the Colorado College Land Company in an attempt to generate revenue for the college. Tenney's brother-in-law, Walter M. Hatch, an attorney from Bloomington Illinois, was employed to administer the Colorado Springs Investment and Improvement Company, a subsidiary of the land company. Tenney & Hatch were able to acquire 960 acres of land in North Cheyenne Cañon and the entrance of South Cheyenne Cañon where they created Colorado College Park and charged 25 cents for admittance and use of the area. Citizen outrage, controversy over the use of the property and delinquent payments on the land forced the sale of 640 acres to the city of Colorado Springs. The Hatches maintained

(Photo of Tenney, Courtesy of Special Collections, Tutt Library, Colorado College, Colorado Springs, Colorado)

control of 320 acres near Helen Hunt Falls, which included a cabin just down from the falls. Conflicting reports question whether the cabin was already on the land or whether it was built by Hatch. Regardless, the Hatch family used it as a

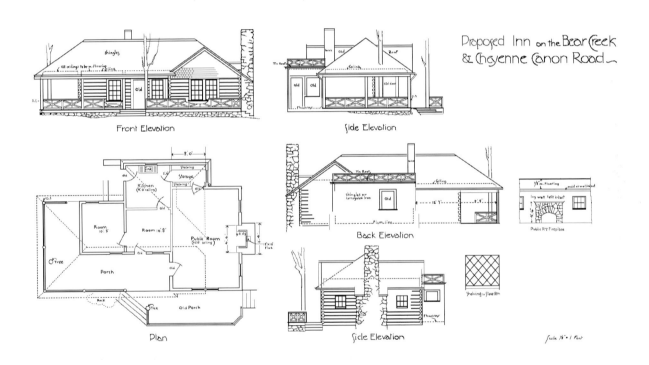

(Original 1903 Bruin Inn Renovation Plans, Courtesy of Special Collections, Tutt Library,

Colorado College, Colorado Springs, Colorado)

second home where they often entertained such guests as Helen Hunt Jackson. Following the bankruptcy of the Colorado College Land Company in 1884, and Hatch's death in 1895, the Hatch cabin along with part of the land was for sale. In 1903, Hatch's wife Mary sold the property for $10,500 to General William J. Palmer, founder of Colorado Springs, through a trustee Joseph F. Lilly who was a partner in the Wright, Lilly & Co. broker investment company. General Palmer renovated the property, in 1903, insisting that there be no destruction of natural vegetation during the renovation. Following the additions to the Hatch cabin the property was given the name Bruin Inn and promptly opened on Saturday the 9th of July, 1904. Envisioning a plan for a *great boulevard system*, General Palmer bought the property to test the concept of a new mountain resort for the area and hired J.E. Lavley to manage the rustic inn. Colorado Springs was "dry" and the intent of General Palmer and other prominent citizens was to found a city based on morals, good taste, and sophistication. The inn was to be a rustic place where visitors could take in the beauty of the area and enjoy an evening of dining and dancing.

In an effort to expand his investment, General Palmer hired architects from Maclaren and Thomas in Colorado Springs to draw plans for an addition to the inn based on sketches by Palmer, on November 14th, 1906, at a cost of $315.00.

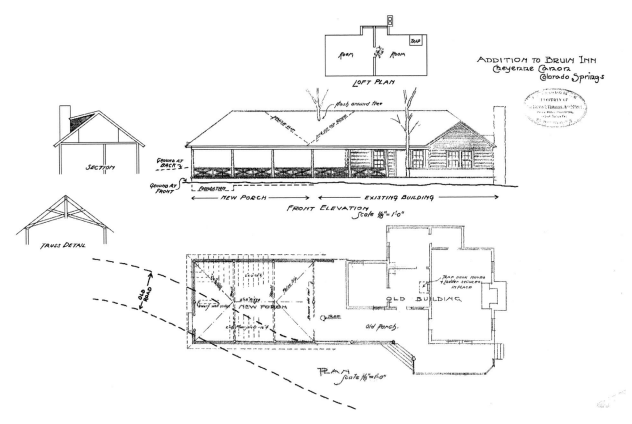

(Original 1906 Bruin Inn Renovation Plans, Courtesy of Special Collections, Tutt Library,

Colorado College, Colorado Springs, Colorado)

According to records, the physical structure had major renovations done three times. Along with renovations came advertising. *"Bruin Inn is just the place for all college parties. Special attention given to large crowds, such as societies and fraternities. Someone in attendance at the inn at all times. Meals served at very reasonable terms.*

Excellent facilities for private dancing parties. J. E. Lavley, Prop." (Colorado College *Tiger* Newspaper, pg. 14 col. 2, December 20th 1907) Advertisements in the college newspaper were consistent and effective based on the number of references by students to the inn in CC yearbooks. Slowly the simple log cabin evolved from nothing more than an experiment and local college hangout and dance hall to a rustic inn serving fine meals and providing quality orchestral music and ballroom dancing. *"The Favorite Resort of the College Students renowned in Story and Song BRUIN INN, Up North Cheyenne Cañon."* (Colorado College *Tiger* Newspaper, pg. 11 col. 1, October 1st 1909)

On the 19th of February 1907 Joseph F. Lilly, Palmer's trustee, quick claim deeded the land to General Palmer for one dollar who in turn deeded the land to the city of Colorado Springs as a gift. Following the change of hands on the property the city leased the Bruin Inn to Mr. Lavley who operated it for a short time before it was leased again for the sum of a little over 3,000 dollars to a Mr. Lee Swanson and Mr. Kenneth F. Riley *"...two energetic and obliging young men of this city. They promise the same treatment accorded to College students by their predecessor..."* (Colorado College *Tiger* Newspaper, pg. 13, col. 2-3, November 5th 1909) Review of numerous CC newspapers and annuals indicates that the Bruin Inn held a special place for many of the students. Through the early years there were two poems and even a song written about the Bruin Inn by the college students.

BRUIN INN
(Words by A. T. French, Music by E. W. Hille.)

"College days are filled with memories,
of the campus, lab and dorm,
Of fraternities and of co-eds,
of cold class-rooms and warm!
We'll remember Deans and Prexy,
all the places where we've been
And we'll recall with rapture
days at dear old Bruin Inn,
Where the little pianola
Gave us many a moonlight tune,
Ah! How dear the farewell visit,
when we came away in June.

CHORUS
When our college days are over
still we'll see them as a dream,
We'll look back again in fancy
and how good they all will seem!
We shall see again old Bruin
and the little waterfall,
The old fireplace a-making
shadow pictures on the wall;
And we can't forget the lunches
eaten there in the days gone by,
The aroma of the coffee,
tender steaks, and apple pie;
When we've thought the whole thing over,
all anew we shall begin
For we ne'er can stop a-dreaming

of our dear old Bruin Inn.
We'll recall the water's ripple
silvery stream in North Cheyenne
Where we used to do our fussing'
with the girl we went with then:
And the many rustic bridges
where we used to sit and spoon
Or more often when we couldn't
ten o'clock came all too soon!
And we'll ask again the question,
is it really such a sin,
If we're just a little tardy
getting home from Bruin Inn?"

(Colorado College Song Booklet, Circa 1910)

(Photo after the 1906 Renovation,
Courtesy of Special Collections, Tutt
Library, Colorado College, Colorado
Springs, Colorado)

Colorado College Fraternities also frequented the inn having group meals and parties celebrating special occasions. *"Bruin Inn was a very popular place on Lincoln's birthday. A large Sigma Chi party spent the morning and ate dinner there, and a Kappa Sigma party the afternoon and evening, winding up with the 'Majestic' afterwards."* (Colorado College *Tiger* Newspaper, pg. 14 col. 2, February 19th 1909)

In addition to the festivities enjoyed by Colorado College students, the inn catered to tourists looking for a place reminiscent of the old west away from the hustle and bustle of city life. In 1914 the proprietors of the Bruin Inn negotiated a contract with the Van Briggle Art Pottery to produce custom art pottery mugs for the restaurant. The mugs, medium brown in color, with the head of a bear carved in low relief on the side were in keeping with the rustic image and name of the inn. Edmund Deforest Curtis, the owner of the Van Briggle Pottery at the time, produced several specialty items for different businesses and organizations. Large orders of these specialty items may have contributed to the pottery not returning to bankruptcy. Emma Kinkead, a young artist who had been affiliated with the Van Briggles and the pottery for several years was primarily responsible for designing the specialty items produced through the early years.

The Bruin Inn continued to thrive and never seemed to loose its appeal or popularity with both tourists and locals. In 1916 a small log cabin was built just below

Helen Hunt Falls as a visitor center and curio shop; its name was the "Cub."
Additionally in 1916, plans were drawn up for the final major renovation to the inn.
Relocation of the chimney and the addition of a large enclosed dance floor were the
main revisions. As the years progressed college students frequented the property much
less allowing it to evolve into a more upscale rustic establishment. *"At the head of*

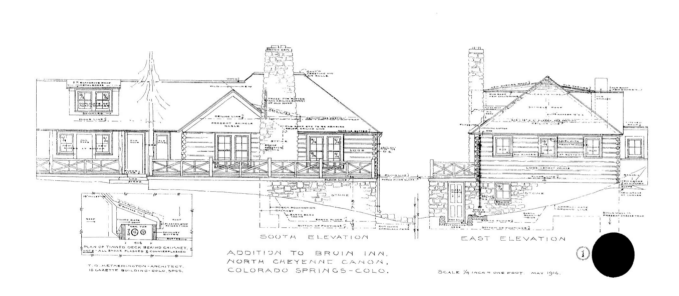

(Original 1916 Bruin Inn Renovation Plans, Courtesy of Special Collections, Tutt Library,

Colorado College, Colorado Springs, Colorado)

North Cheyenne Cañon is Bruin Inn, a spacious rustic inn surrounded with wondrous mountain scenery. Bruin Inn is one of the most popular places in the Pikes Peak

Region for those who wish to enjoy a dinner above the average, and away from the crowd and rush of the city restaurants and hotel dining rooms. There is an excellent dance floor, for those who wish to dance with music by Bruin Inn Novelty Orchestra." (Bruin Inn Advertising Pamphlet, Circa 1940s) On December 13th, 1957, the Bruin

(Bruin Inn Postcard Stamp, Author's Collection)   Inn burned to the ground. Later the city of Colorado Springs relocated the road through where the inn had once stood. Stones

from its foundation were used to build some retaining walls around the road and the words Bruin Inn were spelled out in white quartz and embedded into one wall marking the location of the famed inn.

(Photo of the White Quartz Rocks in North Cheyenne Cañon, Author's Collection)

BRUIN INN, NORTH CHEYENNE CANON.

(Lithograph of North Cheyenne Cañon and the Bruin Inn Circa 1910, Author's Collection)

Club Dinners

Mountain Trout $1.50
Fried Spring Chicken, Family Style $1.50
T-Bone Steak $1.25
Ham and Eggs $1.00

The above orders include French Fried Potatoes, Salad, Hot Biscuits and Marmalade, Coffee, Dessert.

SANDWICHES

May Spread..............................15c
Minced Ham............................15c
Cold Ham................................15c
Fried Ham................................20c
Fried Egg.................................20c
Ham and Egg...........................30c
Cream Cheese.........................15c
Pimento Cheese......................15c
Peanut Butter..........................15c
Bread and Butter.....................10c

PASTRIES

Apple Pie.................................10c
Blueberry Pie...........................15c
Cherry Pie...............................15c
Blackberry Pie.........................10c
Pie a la mode 10c extra

TOAST

French Toast............................40c
Buttered Toast.........................15c
Cinnamon Toast......................20c
Dry Toast.................................10c

Any order served between two persons 10c extra.
Parties with own lunches using tables will be charged.

COLD DRINKS

Coca Cola................................10c   Ice Cream Sundaes..............20c
Pop..10c   Malted Milks........................20c
Sodas......................................10c   Milk Shakes.........................15c
Ice Cream Cones.....................10c   Milk.....................................10c
Ice Cream, Dish.......................15c   Iced Tea..............................10c
Ice Cream Sodas.....................20c

HOT DRINKS

Coffee, per cup........................10c
Chocolate per cup...................10c
Tea per pot..............................10c

We serve banquets and cater to parties of all kinds.

Not responsible for lost articles.

PLEASE PAY WAITER

Bruin Inn Menu Circa 1940s
(Author's Collection)

Bruin Inn Souvenir Flask Circa 1940s

Postcard of the Bruin Inn Interior Circa 1930s

Bruin Inn Postcard Circa 1905

Bruin Inn Collectibles
(Author's Collection)

1908 Colorado College
Barbecue Tumbler
(Author's Collection)

Chapter 3

Barbecue Days at Colorado College

Colorado College, a private liberal arts college established in 1874 in downtown Colorado Springs, was one of the first steps to establishing the town as a prominent location in the state of Colorado. Colorado College had an interesting and prestigious history as well as a close affiliation over the years with the Van Briggle Pottery. Artus Van Briggle came to Colorado Springs in 1899, and befriended several prominent townspeople to include Chemistry Professor William H. Strieby, who provided a small space in his Cutler Hall laboratory, for Van Briggle to work. *"...Professor William Strieby, head of the department of chemistry in Colorado College, himself a deep student of ceramics, who*

(Professor William H. Strieby Photo Courtesy of Special Collections, Tutt Library, Colorado College, Colorado Springs, Colorado)

became much interested in Mr. Van Briggle's experiments. Professor Strieby offered Mr. Van Briggle a corner of his laboratory for a workroom and he began new experiments with dead glazes and Colorado clays..." (Colorado Springs *Gazette,* pg. 7 col. 1-7, December 3rd 1908) From the initial introductions, Colorado College and the Van Briggle Pottery histories continued to crisscross.

Colorado College being a festive and creative school encouraged social and behavioral growth. One event conducted since 1889 was the annual *Barbecue* sponsored by the sophomore class and held on Halloween each year. Because it was one of the most popular yearly events, school members and faculty would often write songs for the occasions.

BARBECUE SONG

"When the autumns leaves are falling
And the green has turned to gold,
Once more the college gathers
As it did in days of old.
But the best time of the season
Is prepared this night for you.
Why? For just the reason
It's '18's Barbecue.
We will one day leave the college
Yet our memory shall remain,
For we have reached the zenith
That a class can e'er attain.
Those who come behind can never,

Though they try it hard to do,
Excel the best one ever –
1918's Barbecue"

(Colorado College Song Book, Circa 1918)

(Photo of Colorado College Football Game Circa 1908, Courtesy of Special Collections,

Tutt Library, Colorado College, Colorado Springs, Colorado)

The barbecue was more than a merry school social event held on Washburn

Field, of Colorado College, where celebrations, singing and dancing prevailed into the night. It was the kickoff preceding the annual Colorado College and Colorado University football game held the following week. The climax of the Halloween event was a large bonfire in the middle of Washburn Field. In 1908 the sophomore class, as in years past, sponsored the annual barbecue, *"BARBEQUE DAYS HAVE COME— Sophs at Work—They Promise to Give More and Spend Less This Year"* (Colorado College *Tiger* Newspaper, pg. 1 col. 3, October 9th 1908). In all the previous years, the bonfire had been the highlight of the barbecue. Each sophomore class had competed to make the fire bigger and better. That effort had taken its toll on Washburn Field causing it to warp out of shape. At about 9:30 p.m. on the night of October 29, 1908 wood that had been collected by the sophomore class for that year's bonfire was set ablaze. The headlines screamed *"1911 FIRE---Unknown culprits started a huge bonfire...fifty men turned out to stop the fierce blaze. About one-third of wood destroyed. Plenty left. Fire bugs had better be scarce."* (Colorado College *Tiger* Newspaper, pg. 1 col. 2, October 30th 1908)

Normally during the annual events a souvenir tin flask for cider was sold to commemorate the event but the sophomore class (graduating class of 1911) decided to change the tradition and offer a Van Briggle tumbler with the date 1911 scripted on it. The pottery produced a simple no handle design utilizing a transparent gloss glaze with the words "BARBECUE CLASS 1911" on one side and interlocking hand carved C's on the opposite. An advertisement describes the event and the souvenir:

"DON'T COME TO THE BARBECUE

Just One Week from Tomorrow
Unless You Want to Have the Time of Your Life
If You Should Happen to Come
You will hear some brand-new C.C. songs, words by French, music by Hille,
You will buy a Van Briggle souvenir stein for the price of one vaudeville show and one
plain soda
You will see the man-in-the-moon get his beard singed.
You will see sundry freshmen go up to see what damage is done.
You will laugh, eat, drink and shiver delightfully.
You will pay fifty cents, if you haven't already"

(Colorado College *Tiger* Newspaper, pg. 11, October 24th 1908)

In past years the barbecue had cost between $1.50 and $2.00 per person but the college administration in 1908 had decided that this amount was extravagant and *"made a ruling"* that the *"subscriptions... should not exceed fifty cents."* (Colorado College *Tiger* Newspaper, pg. 2 col. 1, October 9th 1908) The fifty-cent ticket price covered an evening of all you could eat and all the fun you could stand, and tickets could be purchased from any member of the sophomore class. The October 31st 1908, barbecue featured *"...four novel features"*: *Van Briggle cider mugs, a class salute of eleven bombs, immense numerals of flame on the hillside, hot wienies, all of which made a hit excepting the last."* (Colorado College *Tiger* Newspaper, pg. 1 col. 2, November 6th 1908) There was a capacity crowd that

filled the bleachers in early evening, and a bonfire of 24 feet square at the base and 35 feet high was believed to be the largest bonfire ever, even though one-third of the wood had been destroyed earlier in the week.

(Photo of the Bonfire Woodpile for the Annual Colorado College Barbecue held on October 31" Each Year Circa 1907, Author's Collection)

The program was as follows:

> *"-Welcome...Fowler [Ernest Fowler, Sophomore class president]*
> *-Recitation, "The Frost On the Pumpkin"...S.L. Smith*
> *-Quartet-"Bruin Inn"..... C. Smith, Mailley, Blackman, Warnock*
> *-"From the Faculty Standpoint...President Slocum*
> *-"From the Man Who Has Been Through It"....Shaw*
> *-"Colorado".....Quartet*
> *-"Upward Bound"...C.M. Rose"*
>
> (Colorado College *Tiger* Newspaper, pg. 3 col. 2, November 6th 1908)

Following the program a blanket toss was held with the junior class selecting only *"grievous offenders"* (Colorado College *Tiger* Newspaper, pg. 3 col. 2, November 6th 1908) to throw into the air. A reward of pickles and apples were served to all freshmen that were tossed. The menu that Halloween included *"wienie sandwiches, pickles, doughnuts, peanuts, apples and cider."* (Colorado College *Tiger* Newspaper, pg. 3 col. 2, November 6th 1908) As usual there were complaints about the wienies.

Despite the terrific Barbecue, the CC Tigers lost the football game the following Tuesday in Boulder, 14-0. Coach Richards laid the blame on *"weakness of some essentials of football and lack of confidence in new plays."* (Colorado College *Tiger* Newspaper, pg. 1 col. 1, November 6th 1908) Hope springs eternal and Colorado College looked forward to the game the next year preceded by the annual Halloween barbecue to be sponsored by the class of 1912. They promised to *"knock the spots out of the fizzle."* (Colorado College *Tiger*

Newspaper, pg. 3 col. 2, November 6th 1908) There are no accounts or records of how many of the

Van Briggle tumblers were sold or even produced but the 1908 sophomore class of

Colorado College consisted of 112 students.

(Photo of Cutler Hall at Colorado College Circa 1870s, Courtesy of Special Collections, Tutt Library, Colorado College, Colorado Springs, Colorado)

1909 El Paso Club Mug
(Author's Collection)

Chapter 4

Gentlemen Only

As previously mentioned, Colorado Springs founders wanted a town built on sophistication, prominence, and taste. Five distinguished gentlemen founded an all men's club, The El Paso County Club, on October 23rd 1877. They were Major William Wagner (the city mayor), Dr. Jacob Reed, C. E. Wellsley, E. P. Stephenson and Charles Clark. The original charter consisted of thirty members with some notables being General William J. Palmer founder of Colorado Springs, William S. Jackson husband of famed writer Helen Hunt Jackson, Dr. S. E. Solly promoter of the Manitou Springs water as healing waters, and Charles B. Lansing owner of the Widefield Dairy Ranch and later of the Van Briggle Pottery. Original members paid an initial entrance fee of $5 and a monthly fee of $2. Still in existence, it is believed to be the oldest private town club, west of Chicago. Its original five members envisioned a refined social club; *"a way to get away on an organized basis from their women and other troubles"* (Sprague 212), and insisted on members not carrying firearms during meetings. The club's first president was a respectable man from Philadelphia who had served with General Palmer in the 15th Pennsylvania – Major William Wagner. The club had no permanent residence because locations to assemble were hard to find. Meetings generally were held in the upstairs rooms of downtown buildings around Colorado Springs. The first location used by the club was two rooms on the second floor of the *Gazette* building. The club paid ten dollars a month, which included a

(Photo of Original Colorado Springs *Gazette* Building Circa 1880s, Author's Collection)

water cooler, a copy of the *Gazette*, two card tables and a checkerboard. The privy was a long cold walk so club president Wagner installed one at the top of the stairs. The sixty dollar income from dues did not adequately cover the rent, overhead, breakage, or kerosene for lamps & coal for the pot bellied stove so the club, on May 9th, 1878, moved to cheaper quarters: the upstairs of the First National Bank were rented for five dollars a month.

Colorado College Professor James H. Kerr built a beautiful large home, on the corner of Tejon Street and Platte Avenue, in 1883 near the college campus. The house was a fine Victorian style structure with an ornate interior of black oak woodwork and fine Dutch tile mantels.

(Kerr House Plans Circa 1890 Courtesy of Special Collections, Tutt Library, Colorado College, Colorado Springs, Colorado)

However, after a business deal went sour, causing him to sell a large portion of his assets, he was forced to put his beloved house up for sale. The club, looking at the possibility of finding a permanent home, wanted to buy the house, but there were two issues they needed to resolve. The first was that General Palmer had a liquor covenant in place for the city that was creating problems for the club by misinterpretation from the elected city officials. General Palmer's attitude towards liquor was that public saloons promoted an undesirable type, but occasional "gentleman's" drinks were acceptable. Club members who enjoyed the refreshing taste of whiskey were concerned that sales of liquor on the property were not permitted. This was an important concern because liquor sales were necessary to help maintain the property as well as keeping the members in good spirit. *"Up to then, members had endured the inconvenience of keeping their own liquor supply in private lockers at the Club. After a period of delicate negotiations with Mayor Stillman and ten aldermen, agreement was reached that liquor at the El Paso Club was not liquor in the liquor ban sense."* (Sprague 212)

The second issue was a severe shortage of funds, which would be used to purchase the property and make the necessary changes to meet the club's needs. With technicalities in the liquor law resolved, the club began to sell bonds in September of 1890, attempting to solve the money shortage issue. The asking price of the property was $25,000, which included four lots and the house, with one hundred feet of frontage along Tejon Street and one hundred ninety feet along Platte Avenue. Through the sale of bonds, the men were able to raise enough money to buy the property in 1890, and promptly began setting up the sophisticated club they wanted, with leather chairs and cuspidors in the living room, and a first-rate table covered with all the finest magazines and newspapers to include many college alumni magazines. There was a dining room, which included a bar in the club pantry, and, on the second floor, four rooms for playing cards, and a poolroom. The club rigidly enforced the exclusion of women except for special occasions. On January 25th 1892, a formal opening was held at the club, which brought to order the first official club meeting in the new residence along with a name change. Originally in 1877, the men had wanted to name their new organization The El Paso Club but the name was already taken by another incorporated organization on the outskirts of town. Founding members agreed upon a name modification resulting in The El Paso County Club being formed. By late 1891, the organization using the preferred El Paso Club name ceased to exist. Club officers promptly began proceedings to dissolve The El Paso County Club and re-incorporate as The El Paso Club.

Some founding club members were of English roots. Coupled with a variety of lavish parties and social events, the city earned the nickname of Little London. In the 1890s and early 1900s, the El Paso Club began to change with the influx of many self-made millionaires from the Cripple Creek gold mining community. For these new millionaires, the club was a location to socialize, loosely spend money, conduct business deals over poker and occasionally squabble in an upscale setting.

Many of Colorado Springs' higher class citizens, not to mention many of the club's founders, had a personal association with, provided encouragement, and were instrumental in funding Artus Van Briggle and his new art pottery. Because of this relationship, Van Briggle art pottery was considered fashionable to own. *"A piece of this beautiful ware in your home will stamp you as one possessing rare taste."* (Van Briggle Advertising Catalog, Circa 1912) Through a combination of the club's relationship with the senior pottery staff and the pottery being *in vogue*, the El Paso Club petitioned the Van Briggle Pottery to design a mug for one of their annual dinners, which was held on January 29th 1909. The mug was from the standard pottery line, design 763, and came unglazed in terra cotta. On the side of the mug was the die-impressed imprint "EL PASO CLUB ANNUAL DINNER 1909." The mugs were given to all the club members that year, which totaled somewhere between 100 and 150 regular members. One specific mug was personally signed by several club members during the event and is still on display at the club.

El Paso Mug Signed by Members
During the 1909 Annual Dinner
(El Paso Club Collection)

In 1910, the club made a drastic move and opened a small dining room for women with the addition of a large dining room for the men. In the 1970s, the club and pottery once again crossed paths with the resurgence of interest in the Van Briggle Pottery. In 1977, the pottery produced a bowl glazed in "Russet," a brown matte glaze similar to the old Mountain Crag Brown of the 1920s and 1930s. Engraved on the bowl, in low relief, were the words "EL PASO CLUB" and the bowl was given to guests during the one hundredth anniversary of the club. The pottery also produced another mug for the club in 1977. On October 23rd 1977 a flamboyant party, costing approximately $36,000 was sponsored by the members of the El Paso Club for their

(Photo Courtesy of Colorado Springs Pioneers Museum Starsmore Center For Local History Colorado Springs, CO USA)

one hundredth anniversary – the "Century of Friendship Celebration." This mug was very different from the 1909 annual dinner mug and was made from a more contemporary design with a clear glaze over white clay and a handwritten inscription **"EL PASO CLUB CENTURY OF FRIENDSHIP 1877 – 1977."** Although none of the pieces hold any artistic worth, their production numbers were limited and their historical importance to the city and pottery outweigh their inadequacies.

The club continues operations today with their current membership totaling approximately four hundred, and Colorado Spring's prominent leaders still frequent the establishment that has roots that run deep within the city.

(Photo of the El Paso Club at the corner of Platte Avenue & Tejon Street, Circa 1910, Author's Collection)

1914 Heidelberg Inn Mug
(Author's Collection)

Chapter 5

Bars and Brass Rails

Little known, even among the residents of Colorado Springs, was a town of many less than reputable folks, founded for one purpose – alcohol. Ramona, Colorado, was a town that sprang to life overnight and disappeared almost as fast. Colorado Springs began dry, however Colorado City, just west of Colorado Springs, was as wet as they come. But a combination of greed, politics, prohibitionists, and feuds eventually caused Colorado City to go dry. Colorado City had two factions, one run by Byron Hames and the other by Jim Lacey. Hames, proprietor of the Hotel Hoffman, wanted to just run an honest business selling drinks in the hotel saloon. Lacey, a saloon operator, organized a group of citizens opposing the liquor filled streets of drunks and whores, all the while still wanting to sell liquor, secretly. Lacey's plan was to get alcohol abolished in Colorado City so that he could control the bootlegging industry within the city. Under Lacey's call, prohibitionists gathered support and called an election to vote on whether to go dry or stay wet. The first vote was close with the "wets" winning by 1 vote, however another election was called and the decision was reversed. *"Local option came in, and those in Colorado City who favored prohibition managed to get an election called. The prohibitionists in Colorado City turned out to be unexpectedly numerous, and when the ballots were cast Colorado City remained wet by one vote. But the handwriting on the wall was seen. Another election was called and prohibition carried the day."* (Colorado Springs *Gazette Telegraph*, sec. B pg. 1 col. 1&2, December 19th 1954)

With Colorado City voting to go dry on April 4th, 1911, the "wets" contested the election and appealed the vote in district court. With the uncertainty of becoming dry, city townspeople not in support of the measure began to organize. Two men, Frank L. Wolff and Clarence Kinsman, hatched an idea to start another town; a wet town based on a court ruling on February 10th, 1913, that essentially put the debate to rest in favor of the "dries." Armed with land owned by Mr. Wolff and 20,000 dollars, plans were put into motion to start the new town, but before the town could become official there had to be enough residents to incorporate. Wolff and Kinsman set out to put together a town by starting a petition that would justify incorporation. Forty-nine people signed the petition as residents of the new town, their names were:

James Robert McReynolds   *Lavina E. Donaldson*
Marion Nickell   *Maggie R. Nickell*
Lonnie Nickell   *Hubert C. Thompson*
Mrs. Clara Thompson   *Mrs. Mary C. La Londe*
M.D. Rublee   *George F. Geiger*
Rose A. Geiger   *Emil J. Beck*
W.M. Scott   *Mrs. Nellie Scott*

Mrs Maggie Moats	L.C. Moats
Pleasant L. Allen	J. M. Hunnel
Sarah A. Hunnel	G.E. Wetherwax
Mary D Wetherwax	C.W. Shapley
Mrs Nellie M. Shapley	G.C. Wiseman
S.E. Williams	J.C. Irvin
Nellie Irvin	Mary H Allen
C. Allen	Mary Geising
Henry Geising	George Geising
John Sholes	William Hicks
Elmer Eggert	Frank C. Wolff
C. Limsky	J.C. McCreary
W.H. Abbey	Mae Mantz
Philomena O'Brien	C.E. Bishop
C.D. Taylor	John Dwyer
Lou A Carter	Mabelle A. Carter
H.A. Jordan	Bertha Jordan
S. Kranz	

(Petition to Incorporate the Township of Ramona, Jul. 17th 1913)

Colorado City, disgusted with the proposal, moved to stop the incorporation. *"The dry element in Colorado City, not especially pleased at their plans, made an effort to have Ramona annexed and asked for an injunction to prevent the incorporation."* (Colorado Springs *Gazette,* pg. 7 col. 6&7, October 26th 1913) Judge W. F. Kinney approved the petition to incorporate on July 29th, 1913, and ordered James McReynolds, George Geiger &

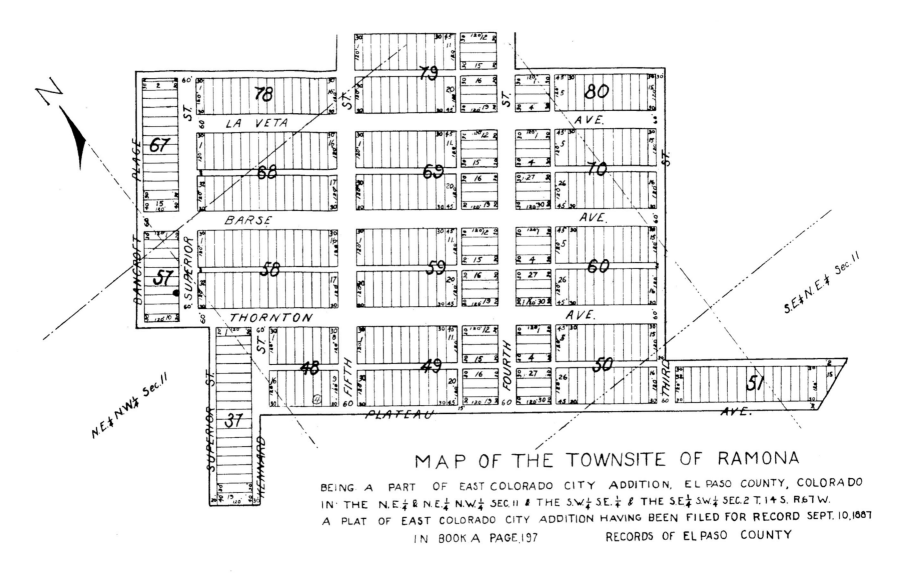

MAP OF THE TOWNSITE OF RAMONA

BEING A PART OF EAST COLORADO CITY ADDITION, EL PASO COUNTY, COLORADO
IN THE N.E.¼ & N.E.¼ N.W.¼ SEC. 11 & THE S.W.¼ S.E.¼ & THE S.E.¼ S.W.¼ SEC. 2 T. 14 S. R.67 W.
A PLAT OF EAST COLORADO CITY ADDITION HAVING BEEN FILED FOR RECORD SEPT. 10, 1887
IN BOOK A PAGE 197   RECORDS OF EL PASO COUNTY

(Ramona Town Plot Circa 1913, Courtesy of Colorado Springs Pioneers Museum Starsmore Center for Local History Colorado Springs, CO USA)

H. C. Thompson as interim commissioners until a formal election could vote on incorporation. Wolff and Kinsman won and on August 21st, 1913, the town of Ramona came into existence. A small 360-acre tract of land just six blocks north of Colorado City became the town. The first order of business conducted was an ordinance authorizing the sale of liquor. *"...saloon buildings were hastily moved there or constructed. Bars and brass rails were toted over to the place and there a new oasis was established."* (Colorado Springs *Gazette Telegraph*, sec. B pg. 1 col. 1&2, December 19th 1954).

Ramona was for drinking, the residents knew it, and advertised it as such. *"Ramona, the new booze annex to Colorado City, opened Monday night in a blaze of glory, and, according to the papers, 'carriages met the cars at Fourth street to carry patrons.' But were the carriages on hand to haul them home after the festivities ended?"* (Colorado City *Iris*, Nov. 21st 1913) Ramona consisted of a town mayor, marshal, town council, jail, athletic club, dairy, and a handful of other businesses besides saloons. The town even built a small arena for boxing and wrestling matches. Despite Ramona's attempt to act and look conventional, Colorado City and Colorado Springs were sickened with the new town. On January 2nd, 1914, Colorado Springs refused water permits for Ramona businesses. *"...it is a moral cesspool in which the perverts, bums, saloonkeepers and other riffraff of the county have assembled to make their last stand."* (Colorado Springs *Gazette*, pg. 8 col. 1, October 30th 1914) Outraged, Ramona took the city of

Colorado Springs to court to force the issue. Colorado Springs argued that if Ramona could sell liquor how and to whom they wanted why could they not do the same with their water? Ramona eventually lost the court battle, and on February 3rd, 1914, Colorado Springs cut-off all water to businesses in the township. In an effort to bypass the ruling, the town marshal, Lennie Moats, began wheeling a water tank down to Colorado City each evening and would fill the tank from the street fire hydrants.

One such business in the town was the largest saloon, known as the Heidelberg Inn. The owners, George and Rose Geiger, ran the inn until statewide prohibition took effect on January 1st, 1916. George, one of the few reputed upstanding citizens in Ramona, was also the town mayor from 1914 through 1916. *"Mr. & Mrs. George Geiger entertained all of their former employees and a number of friends with a big turkey dinner at the Heidelberg Inn on the evening of January 1st. The big spread was prepared by Mrs. Geiger and George did the serving himself, and those present say he is about the finest ever."* (Colorado City *Iris,* Jan. 6th 1916) The Geiger's took pride in their establishment with fine decorating, quality service and upscale serving ware. One way they achieved this was to incorporate Van Briggle items into their business. The pottery designed a Heidelberg Inn mug, based on a mug from the pottery's regular line, design 28B. It is not known how many of these mugs they made, or even how many survived

(Heidelberg Inn on right side of 4th Street in Ramona Colorado Circa 1915, Photo Courtesy of Colorado Springs Pioneers Museum Starsmore Center for Local History Colorado Springs, CO USA)

the short existence of the Heidelberg Inn, but they are extremely rare.

In 1916 statewide prohibition took hold and what started as a grand idea was over at the stroke of a pen. Frank Burnett and Bill O'Neal leased the Heidelberg Inn for a short time from George Geiger, and tried to keep the business open as a restaurant holding periodic fights and boxing contests. Ramona attempted to continue as a

(Postcard Showing the Interior View of the Heidelberg Inn Circa 1914, Author's Collection)

legitimate town, but since the majority of its revenue was based on saloons it soon faded away. *"No more will the musician sit before the piano at Ramona and tickle the ivories, while men line up before the bar and keep time with the clink of glasses. No more will Colorado City officials be required to spend most of their time at the corner of Fourth and Colorado Avenue to act as a steering committee to pass the booze soaked hides, on down the line to Colorado Springs. The oasis has vanished from the desert and the thirsty souls must go to greener pastures or be satisfied with H2O."* (Colorado City *Iris*, Jan. 6th 1916). On January 16th, 1919, the United States ratified the 18th Amendment to the Constitution essentially putting the final nail in the coffin for the town. Thorndale Park was laid out making the former *"wild side"* a more traditional neighborhood.

"Now the people up there can settle down to peace and quiet, can boost and boom that location as a beautiful residence site, a place for homes, where scenery and beauty are before the eyes at all times, for this location commands the best view of the mountains to be had in the entire district." (Colorado City *Iris*, Jan. 6th 1916) On April 1st, 1947, residents of the town of Ramona voted to

(Heidelberg Inn Trade Token Circa 1915, Author's Collection)

disincorporate ending a little known piece of Colorado history with a vote of 46 to 4.

L to R Top Row: 1914 Half Way House/Sigma Chi Mug, 1907 - 1912 Kappa Sigma Mug, 1907 - 1912 Phi Gamma Delta Mug
L to R Bottom Row: 1907 - 1912 Kappa Sigma Mug, 1916 Phi Gamma Delta Mug
(Author's Collection)

Chapter 6

Greeks

Colorado College's association with the Van Briggle Art Pottery has been widely linked from the earliest days of the pottery to the college's eventual purchase of the memorial pottery building in 1968. Another such association was with fraternal organizations of the college. As various fraternity chapters were activated on the Colorado College campus in the early 1900s, their histories eventually overlapped with the pottery giving a glimpse into their past.

Between 1904 and 1914, five national social fraternities activated chapters at Colorado College: Beta Theta Pi (ΒΘΠ) Gamma Delta chapter, Kappa Sigma (ΚΣ) Beta Omega chapter, Phi Delta Theta (ΦΔΘ) Colorado Beta chapter, Phi Gamma Delta (ΦΓΔ) Chi Sigma chapter, and Sigma Chi (ΣΧ) Beta Gamma chapter. Of the five, at least three were directly affiliated with the Van Briggle Pottery through specialty items that were produced for the fraternities. In addition, many of the fraternities frequented some of the other local establishments, that had direct ties to the Van Briggle Pottery.

Kappa Sigma, the oldest Colorado College fraternity, has had, at least, 4 different specialty items produced by the pottery for fraternity members over the years. One, a specialty mug, was from a design out of the regular pottery line glazed in a matte lime green glaze with gold Greek lettering painted on the side . This particular mug was produced some time between 1907 and 1912, based on bottom markings. Indications are that the mug was not produced for any specific event but more as a commemorative item for fraternity members in general. Another example of the fraternity mugs was a larger version

similar in color

and markings and

also from the same

time period. It is

not definitively

known if the mugs

were produced

during the same

year or even the

same firing but

based on glaze

(Photo of CC Football Game & Kappa Sigma Car, Undated Photo Courtesy of Special Collections, Tutt Library, Colorado College, Colorado Springs, Colorado)

colors both inside and out along with the gold letter markings on the exterior, there is a very good possibility that they were. The next item was a small log cabin incense burner given to Kappa Sigma alumni during the annual dance held at the Broadmoor Hotel in 1922. The log cabin was a standard pottery specialty item used to denote a variety of special events and organizations through the 1920s. Several examples have surfaced, both marked and unmarked. The fourth item was a three-inch circular paperweight depicting the fraternity coat of arms and glazed in the Ming turquoise glaze. This particular item was made in the late 1920s to early 1930s, and seems to have been a somewhat common item some other fraternities used.

Phi Gamma Delta, another fraternity that still exists today, also had a consistent relationship with the Van Briggle Pottery. At least three varieties of specialty items were produced for this fraternity between the years of 1907 and 1916. Each of the three mugs is of a different design and markings making the dating process somewhat easier.

Confusion over two variations of the fraternal coat of arms, on two of the mugs, led to research on its evolution. The heraldic insignia of the Phi Gamma Delta fraternity changed numerous times from the late nineteenth century through the mid teens of the twentieth century. Versions depicted on the Van Briggle mugs match the evolutionary track of the coat of arms based on the time period the mugs were made. The first mug is one that was located at the Pioneers Museum in Colorado Springs.

The mug is design 28B from the regular pottery line glazed in a curdled matte purple glaze with gold Phi Gamma Delta Greek lettering painted on the side, similar to the Kappa Sigma mugs. The second mug had a design change with a new larger stein version along with a graphic transfer depicting one of three or four coat of arms used after 1902. The mug design is 763 from the regular pottery line glazed in a clear gloss with an image affixed to the outside of the mug. Both mugs one and two are from the 1907 – 1912 period but it is unclear which came first. In 1913, the Ecclesia began deliberations to clarify and agree upon one coat of arms for the fraternity. Modifications continued until one standard was established, however the standardization would only last a short time before a minor modification took hold. The emblem has remained unchanged to the present day. The third mug found is from 1916 and depicts the final coat of arms. Of all the Phi Gamma Delta specialty items designed by the pottery the 1916 version is the most artistic. The mug design, again, a variation of 28B used in earlier years, with the fraternity coat of arms carved in low relief on the side of the mug, is glazed in a dark blue matte. One example found has a heavily faded handwritten or painted saying on the side, *PELing Pug '19.* Perhaps it was a nickname given to a fraternity member at that time with either their year of graduation, sports number, or secret fraternal number.

Sigma Chi, still another fraternity that exists today, had at least two specialty items produced by the pottery. One of the two items is by far the most unique of all the Colorado College fraternity mugs, not only because of the detailed design but the relationship between the college and an area establishment. A specialty mug, produced for the fraternity, was a modified design from the regular pottery line, glazed in matte blue, with the Sigma Chi heraldic symbol displayed on the side of the mug along with a high relief area revealing the words "Half Way House 1914" on the side. This particular mug was produced in 1914 based on bottom markings and the illustration on the side of the mug. Indications are that the mug commemorated a specific event for fraternity members. Discussions with noted author and Half Way House historian, Mike Doty, indicate the mug is indeed rare and provides a unique and relatively unknown relationship between Colorado College fraternities and the Half Way House on Pikes Peak. The second item is a three-inch circular paperweight, similar to the Kappa Sigma version, depicting the fraternity coat of arms and glazed in the Ming turquoise glaze. This particular item was also made in the late 1920s to early 1930s.

To date, no known examples of specialty items for either the Beta Theta Pi and Phi Delta Theta fraternities have been uncovered, and the two fraternities no longer have active chapters at Colorado College, which makes locating items even more difficult. However, since both of these fraternities activated chapters in the early teens of the twentieth century, at Colorado College, it makes sense why no pre-1910 examples have been located as with the other fraternities. Nevertheless, due to the colleges past affiliation with the pottery and numerous specialty items surfacing, it is safe to assume there were examples produced at some point, for the two aforementioned fraternities, which still reside in private collections or alumni estates. Regardless, any specialty items produced for the Colorado College fraternities were made in extremely small quantities and while only a handful of them express any true artistic merit; their rarity and scarcity make them highly sought after among Van Briggle collectors.

1922 Kappa Sigma Smoker
(Todd Sutherland Collection)

1920/30s Sigma Chi Paperweight
(Collection of Bob Teas &
Kathy Honea)

1907 - 1912 Phi Gamma Delta Mug
(Photo Courtesy of Colorado Springs Pioneers
Museum Starsmore Center for Local History
Colorado Springs, CO USA)

1920/30s Kappa Sigma Paperweight
(Author's Collection)

1914 Colorado College
Sigma Chi/Half Way House Mug
(Author's Collection)

Chapter 7

Along the Cog Road

In 1878, Edward and Manville Booth acquired 320 acres of land through the Homestead Act of 1862 in a small canyon near the junction of Ruxton and South Ruxton Creeks along the present-day Pikes Peak Cog Railway. Following the land acquisition, the Booth brothers built a one-room cabin on the property some time prior to 1882 where the brothers ran cattle in the summer months. In August of 1883, the brothers sold the property to William A. Richards who owned it for only a year primarily, because his wife refused to live in such an austere and remote location. Respecting his wife's wishes, Richards boarded up the cabin and relocated the family prior to selling it on August 7th, 1884.

In the spring of 1884, Thomas T. Palsgrove signed a contract to pack supplies for the construction of a new army signal station at the summit of Pikes Peak. Palsgrove led a caravan of twelve burros loaded with supplies once a day to the top of the mountain until the job was complete. While making the journey, Palsgrove frequently passed by an abandoned cabin in a small valley surrounded by hills on three sides that was located near a beautiful waterfall. He instantly fell in love with the setting and after much

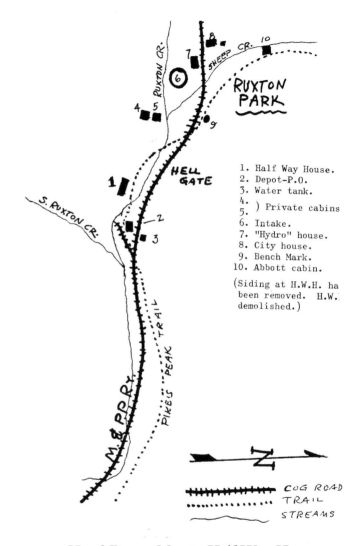

Pre 1906 Half Way House Advertising Card
(Author's Collection)

Hand Drawn Map to Half Way House
(Courtesy of Bill Abbott)

discussion with his wife, Nettie, they agreed to purchase the property. Negotiations with Richards allowed Palsgrove to purchase the land relatively inexpensively, due to his eagerness to sell, and setting the stage for Palsgrove's next profession – innkeeper. Immediately, he began to improve the property by repairing damaged furniture, building a corral and stable for the cow, constructing rudimentary bridges across the creeks and eventually building additions onto the cabin.

Almost by accident, Palsgrove found himself playing host to climbers and transients moving through the area, so he decided to run a bunkhouse/inn. As a proprietor of an inn, he gave the business the name *Pikes Peak Trail House*, but later changed it to *Half Way House*. This name was somewhat misleading to travelers since the location of the inn was approximately two and a half miles up the cog road from the present day cog railway station. *"Palsgrove's place was only a quarter of the way from Manitou, but he could hardly have been expected to call it the Quarter Way House."* (Abbott 194) Continued improvements expanded the inn allowing in excess of fifteen rooms for rent that seemed to consistently stay leased, with some guests reserving rooms for the entire summer.

In the late 1880s, the Manitou & Pikes Peak Railway was constructed, and on the 16th of August 1890 the first train reached the Half Way House. The Palsgroves enjoyed some privileges they had negotiated when granting a right of way through their

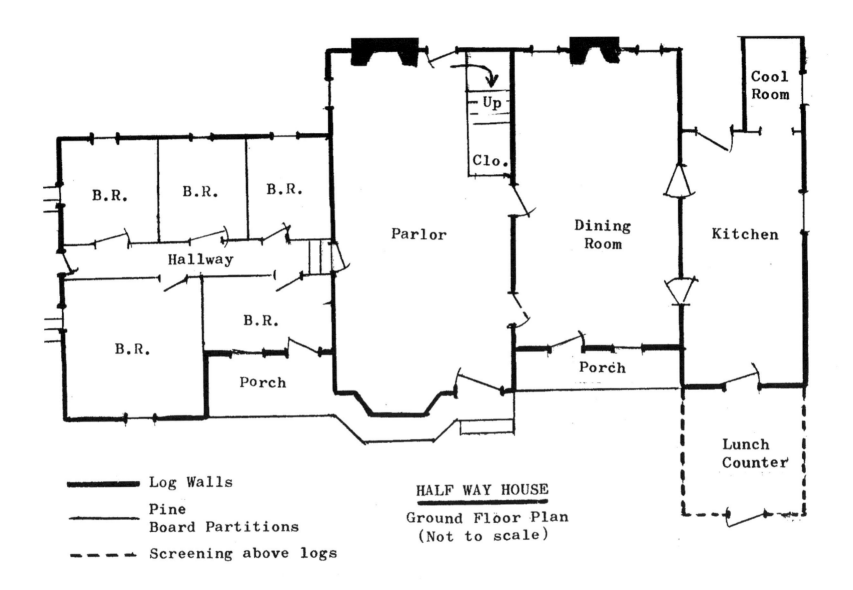

B.R.

B.R.

B.R.

Up

Clo.

Cool
Room

Hallway

Parlor

Dining
Room

Kitchen

B.R.

B.R.

Porch

Porch

Lunch
Counter

Log Walls

Pine
Board Partitions

Screening above logs

HALF WAY HOUSE
Ground Floor Plan
(Not to scale)

Half Way House Floor Plan
(Courtesy of Bill Abbott)

property. They were given free cog railway transit for life to all family members, and the addition of a US Post Office. More construction was done to include a small depot located at the track split near the junction of Ruxton and South Ruxton Creeks just down from the inn. Palsgrove also built Nokomis Lodge, which housed a bowling alley, shooting gallery, and billiard room; none of which ever caught on.

With the ease of movement into and out of the Half Way House, the Palsgroves saw an influx of business. Palsgrove had purchased twenty-five burros for taking guests on local excursions. Additionally, the location was a resting stop for companies in Manitou who ran guided burro tours to the summit of Pikes Peak. Visitors frequented the establishment and the Palsgrove family took advantage of the tourism by selling souvenirs such as local minerals, Navajo rugs, wild flowers and postcards. Tourists or guests who bought postcards could have them postmarked at the Half Way House Post Office and taken by mule down to Manitou. Mail delivery ran every day except Sunday. Establishment of the post office also led to the creation of the exclusive Half Way Colorado mail cancellation stamp.

(Half Way Colorado Cancellation Stamp, Author's Collection)

Following the sale of a majority stake in the property, Tom and Nettie Palsgrove moved away and eventually sold all their interests in the Half Way House. John B. Palsgrove, Tom's brother, managed the Half Way House for a number of years for an Omaha investment group after Tom sold out. Eventually, John and his wife Jennie purchased the property back and continued to run a successful business, living and working at the inn. Over the years however, John and Jennie began to drift apart, possibly from the stresses associated with living such a rustic life, and on November 9th, 1906, they filed for divorce. In the settlement, Jennie retained control of the property and continued to operate the inn with the help of Jennie's brother-in-law and half sister, Frank & Katie Gunn.

The Gunn's helped Jennie Palsgrove keep the inn running smoothly until a terrible accident occurred, on the 1st of August 1907, leaving the Gunns in control of the property. Conflicting accounts recorded the accident; one listed Mrs. Palsgrove as having been struck by lightning and the other recounting her incident as electrocution when she attempted to shut off a single light bulb in the laundry room of the inn. Regardless, she died instantly and the event left a permanent mark on guests of the inn. *"A special train came up from Manitou for her body...the spectacle of that little engine, throwing sparks high into the air, as it came puffing up the hill to the Half Way House depot."* (Abbott 198)

Following the death of Mrs. Palsgrove, controlling interest of the inn changed hands several times all while the Gunns attempted to run the business; unfortunately Katie Gunn was not much of a cook *"...the fare left much to be desired.."* (Abbott 198) Around 1910, a family from Missouri leased the property for $800 per year. William H. Harris and his family renovated the inn with many needed improvements and began to try and rebuild the reputation of the once popular establishment. For the most part they succeeded by giving more attention to transitory guests versus regular tenants. The entire family worked hard to ensure the success with Mr. & Mrs. Harris' children doing a great deal of the chores and extracurricular activities associated with the inn.

Successes of the Bruin Inn were highly publicized in their willingness to cater to the students of Colorado College, so the Harris family, recognizing the market,

(Photo of the Interior of the Half Way House Parlor, Courtesy of Bill Abbott)

attempted to solicit the college's business. They hosted special events but never to the magnitude that the Bruin Inn achieved. On the 24th of April 1915 the Contemporary Society at Colorado College held its annual function at the Half Way House. It was *"...a unique outing which took the form of a hike from the top of Mt. Manitou and an elaborate dinner party at the Half Way house. The members and guests went to Manitou in a special car and from there were conveyed by the incline to the top of Mt. Manitou."* (Colorado College *Tiger* Newspaper, pg. 3 col. 4, April 27th 1915)

Another indication that special events took place at the inn was with the discovery of a Colorado College fraternity mug, produced by the Van Briggle Pottery, specifically designed with the Half Way House name impressed in high relief along with the date. No indications point to any one particular event where the mug was given out to fraternity members during the 1914 school year. The Half Way House might have in some way sponsored the fraternity or the inn might have kept the mugs to promote a special relationship between the inn and fraternity members during 1914. Nevertheless, the mug is extremely rare. There are only two known examples to exist.

In an attempt to control its watershed, the city of Colorado Springs purchased the Half Way House and surrounding property on the 20th of October 1916. The Harris family could still lease the property and continued to operate the inn until its eventual closure. On November 23rd, 1921, the Half Way House closed its doors for the final time. In January of 1922, hikers using the abandoned cabin started a fire in the living room fireplace. A log rolled out of the fireplace and accidentally caught the living room floor on fire, however only minor damage occurred. Following the fire, the structure remained empty until 1926 when the inn was finally dismantled and the wood used to build a workers' construction camp at Big Tooth Reservoir. Today only small trees, shrubs, and a rock foundation remain of the site where the Half Way House once stood closing the chapter on a hidden gem along the cog railway.

Various Half Way House Photos
Clockwise from Upper Left:
Circa 1906 - 1910 Photo,
Circa 1888 - 1905 Hook Photo,
Circa 1912 - 1921 Photo
(Author's Collection)

Various Recovered Half Way House Artifacts
Clockwise from Lower Left:
Piece of Broken Plate,
Portion of a Kerosene Lamp,
Piece of Broken Plate
(Author's Collection)

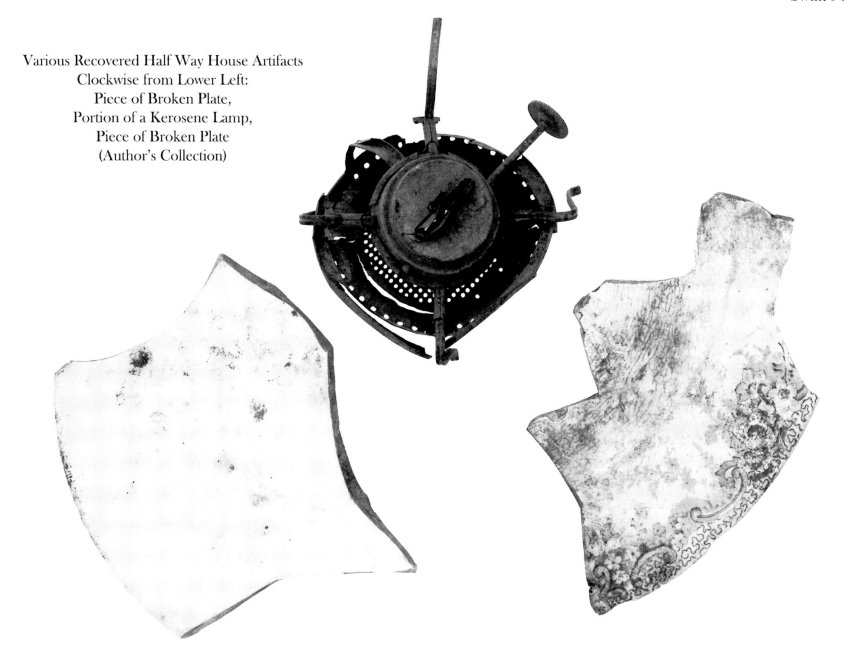

1914 Mission Inn Chamberstick
(Photo Courtesy of Rago Arts & Auction
Center/Lambertville NJ)

1914 Mission Inn Pitcher
(Photo Courtesy of Richard Sasicki)

1914 Mission Inn Tumbler
(Photo Courtesy of the Van Briggle Pottery)

Chapter 8

Mission of Bells

In 1874, Christopher Columbus Miller arrived in the infant city of Riverside, California. Miller was a civil engineer who had come to the city to work on a water system. By 1876, when the project was complete, Miller received payment for services in the form of a large lot in the heart of downtown Riverside. He and his family built an adobe two-story boardinghouse called the Glenwood and found themselves in the hotel business. C.C. Miller's oldest son was Frank Augustus Miller, who, having tried several other enterprises bought the adobe building and property from his father for $5000. After Frank's marriage, he began to work on a grand hotel for the growing California town, but money was in short supply. By 1902, he was only able to build a U-shaped four-story facility around a courtyard in typical Spanish style. Regardless, the hotel was a success.

As the years went on, he added three wings. In 1910, the Cloister Wing with guest rooms, gift shop, St. Cecilia's Chapel, and a large music room were built. An area called the Catacombs or the Cloister Walk was a major tourist draw. It featured nooks, chambers and art objects but is now closed to the public. Some of the items that would have been sold in the Cloister Wing gift shop were Van Briggle Pottery drinking glasses,

Cloister Art Shop, Glenwood Mission Inn, Riverside, California.

(Photo of the Mission Inn Cloister Art Shop, Author's Collection)

candlesticks and pitchers. The pieces were a dark speckled brown matte finish with a mission bell in low relief. The words "MISSION INN" were spelled out below the bell on each piece. The owner of the Van Briggle Pottery, Edmund Curtis, was marketing aggressively all over the country, attempting to keep the Van Briggle Pottery afloat. Perhaps this would explain why this California hotel sold Colorado pottery.

The Spanish Wing was added in 1913-14 to include a patio similar to those found in Spanish castles. Frank's growing art collection necessitated the addition of an art gallery in that wing. In the 1920s two more floors were added to the hotel and the International Rotunda Wing was completed in 1931. The International Wing included an oriental area for Frank Miller's eastern interests. Following the additions, the

(Mission Inn Bronze Bell Collectible, Circa 1913, Private Collection)

building filled out the entire city block in downtown Riverside and included gardens, towers, archways and stairways.

During its early glory years, famous people from all walks of life came to stay in The Mission Inn. Theodore Roosevelt and Andrew Carnegie both visited the hotel, and Sarah Bernhardt stayed there after her performance at the Riverside Opera House. Royalty from Sweden, Russia, and Japan were entertained at banquets, but Miller's death in 1935 set off a decline in the hotel's fortunes. By 1956 the Miller family had sold the hotel. Times and interests were changing -- the Depression, new tourist interests, and the move from urban areas led to twenty years of neglect which caused a loss of much art work and the hotel falling into a state of general disrepair. Finally in 1976 the Riverside Redevelopment Corporation bought the once proud lady. In 1985 the hotel was to close for a two-year renovation but a developer's bankruptcy caused the two years to extend to seven and one-half years of closure. On December 30, 1992, the grand old Mission Inn was finally reopened to the public.

Managed by the Mission Inn Foundation, the hotel boasts a museum filled with its history and aided by the Friends of the Mission Inn. Listing on the National Register of Historic Places protects it from former kinds of abuse. The mission bell symbol or rain cross appears on the pieces of pottery made and has become the Mission Inn symbol in honor of the Millers and their interest in collecting bells. At one time the Mission Inn was referred to as the "Mission of Bells." The Mission Inn became a grand collection of art and architecture begun by the Miller family.

(www.missioninnmuseum.com)

(Photo of the Mission Inn, Circa 2004)   (Postcard of the Mission Inn, Circa 1920)

1919 Reserve Watch Plaque
(Author's Collection)

Chapter 9

The Boys Back Home

In June 1914, Austrian Archduke Francis Ferdinand was assassinated in Sarajevo, Bosnia plunging Europe into World War I. Following repeated U-boat attacks on unarmed supply ships, President Woodrow Wilson asked Congress to declare war on Germany, on April 2nd, 1917. The declaration was passed on April 6th, 1917, and the first full national draft called all able-bodied men to serve their country. *"With only 128,000 men in the regular Army the U.S. required all men from 21 to 30 to register for military service. The age range was broadened to 18-45 in 1918. A lottery determined who served."* Although *"the U.S. armed forces had almost 5 million men and women by the end of the war,"* (http://www.aolsvc.worldbook.aol.com) many others wished to serve in some other way.

In Colorado Springs, those men that were unable to pass the draft restrictions could serve in an organization called the Reserve Watch. In many American communities, citizens were worried about new foreign enemies and wanted the protection of local volunteer guard groups. Mayor Charles E. Thomas and the city council sponsored the Reserve Watch.

A photograph, during a World War I victory day parade, indicates that Reserve Watch members wore dark jackets and pants. Additionally, it was known that the watch members wore a bronze shield or button that read *"Colorado Springs Reserve Watch."* Initially they were only able to carry nightsticks and pocketknives because factories could not turn out new guns for the war fast enough. First to receive the rifles were the regular army, then the reserves, and finally home guard groups like the Reserve Watch. On June 8th, 1917, the *Gazette* reported that the army had authorized the Reserve Watch to carry army rifles as soon as they were available. The city was divided into eight wards with a Captain, Lieutenant, and three sergeants organizing each ward. The units drilled weekly at a field in their ward with or without weapons. Among the participants, the *Gazette* listed prominent citizen, Charles L. Tutt, as a corporal in Ward One.

The job of the organization was to fill in for the soldiers that had gone to war. They were asked to patrol the streets for special events such as the July 4th, 1917 parade. The regular police were deployed along the parade route, and a portion of the Reserve Watch took up the slack in patrolling the remainder of the town. During the winter of 1917, these men, many of wealth and position, also protected the grain elevators in Colorado Springs. The men stood guard in four-hour shifts in the freezing weather. They carried *"revolvers and riot guns and patrolled the dark corners of the railroad yards where the wheat elevators"* were. (Colorado Springs *Gazette*, pg. 4 col. 1, December 13th 1917)

"Lawyers, brokers, doctors, business men of all lines, compose the relief and devote half their night once or twice a month to a task which not only is thankless and arduous, but is by no means devoid of danger." (Colorado Springs *Gazette*, pg. 4 col. 1, December 13th 1917) Perhaps their most exciting endeavor was involvement in capturing the Dale gang that was escaping from the Denver area. *"Reserve Watch members set up roadblocks at more than 50 locations"* on September 16th, 1918. (Colorado Springs *Gazette*, pg. 4 col. 1, September 17th 1918) The criminals were finally captured in Sedalia.

By the latter part of 1918, the war was coming to an end and the need for a home guard was declining. Nevertheless, the organization marched in the victory day parade following the end of the war. On September 14th, 1919, the organization was disbanded with the promise that they would return should emergencies in the city arise. A special disbandment day included an afternoon of shooting, followed by a dinner at the new Jewett Memorial Field and clubhouse (later to become the Patty Jewett Golf Course.) There was music, speeches and *"a pleasant evening around the fireplace"*. (Colorado Springs *Gazette*, pg. 7 col. 2, September 14th 1919) Each retiring member received what the *Gazette* called a *"handsome ash tray of Van Briggle Pottery, bearing the insignia of the organization."* (Colorado Springs *Gazette*, pg. 7 col. 2, September 14th 1919)

A rabbit shoot in 1921 was to reduce a perceived surplus of jackrabbits and cottontails. The Reserve Watch was divided into two teams with the losers paying for dinner for the winners. The dead rabbits became food for Associated Charities. This was to be an annual event but there is no record of any further activities, and so the Colorado Springs Reserve Watch passed into history.

(Photo of the Reserve Watch Victory Day Parade, Courtesy of Pikes Peak Library District & Stewarts Commercial Photographers)

1914 Yale University Fraternity
of Book and Bond Mug
(Author's Collection)

Chapter 10

Book and Bond

On October 14th, 1899, Benjamin F Nead approached E. H. Berner, both Yale University students, about the need for a secret fraternal organization; a fraternal organization *"...which should stand for the university's true democratic principles."* (Undated Papers, Records of Book and Bond) Both believing the new fraternity was a good idea, they conducted a meeting with two other students, George M. Baker and Irving C. Bull, soliciting their opinions of the idea. All agreed and promptly began writing a constitution by which the fraternity would live. Following the completion and confirmation of the constitution, on April 5th, 1900, three additional people were brought into the new secret society: Harry H. Read, Edwy L. Taylor and Herbert B. North. On May 2nd, 1900, the new fraternity had a meeting with Yale President Arthur T. Hadley to convince him of the virtue of the idea. President Hadley agreed and the new organization became official, and was known as *"Fraternity of Book and Bond."* (Undated Papers, Records of Book and Bond) Also known by its lesser-used names of Phi Kappa Epsilon and Ammanot Club, the fraternity began to design a fraternal symbol, and on May 10th, 1900, agreed upon a design proposed by Irving C. Bull; *"...a raised gold pin in the form of a book, surrounded by a raised, buckled, gold strap with the letters ΦKE*

engraved there upon; signifying, a secret student body, bound together by an

unbreakable bond." (Undated Papers, Records of Book and Bond)

Book and Bond

(1911 Initiation Banquet Program, Records of Book and Bond)

The new fraternity, considered quite upstanding citizens, held meetings every

Thursday from 8:30 PM until midnight. They followed strict by-laws, prohibited

alcohol, or even alcoholic ingredients in food prepared for banquets. Members were

required to wear, except for social functions, dark suits, black shoes, black socks, white

shirts with stiff collars, black ties, and derby hats. The uniform was meant to *"...foster a*

spirit of unity among members." (Undated Papers, Records of Book and Bond) Fraternity officers

also fined members fifty cents for missing weekly meetings. In addition to the strict by-

laws, secrecy was of the utmost importance, meeting bulletins stated, *"destroy after reading.*" (Undated Papers, Records of Book and Bond) The fraternity even had its own code for writing secret correspondence:

1 = H	*11 = R*	*22 = B*
2 = I	*12 = S*	*23 = C*
3 = J	*13 = T*	*24 = D*
4 = K	*14 = U*	*25 = E*
5 = L	*15 = V*	*26 = F*
6 = M	*16 = W*	*27 = G*
7 = N	*17 = X*	*and = +*
8 = O	*18 = Y*	*the = √*
9 = P	*19 = Z*	*but = ◉*
10 = Q	*20 = etc.*	*us = :*
of = ⊥	*21 = A*	*to = -*
into = ÷	*secret = Δ*	*when = ＜*
book and bond = {}	*fraternity = ΦKE*	*constitution = ▢*
graduate council = θ	*special meeting = ♀*	

(i.e. The fraternity of Book and Bond is having success)
(√, ΦKE, ⊥, {}, 2, 12, 1, 21, 15, 2, 7, 27, 12, 14, 23, 23, 25, 12, 12)
(Rudd 1)

Pledging was very selective and no freshmen were solicited until after they had completed at least five months at the university. Every spring and fall, initiations were held in the chamber of mysteries where meticulous, almost Gothic, ceremonies were performed for new members. A 1903 handwritten description outlines the initiation ritual:

All initiations shall take place in the Chamber of Mysteries of the Society, in utter silence except for the directions and responses. The Chamber of Mysteries shall be lighted only by a small, well shaded light placed on a table in the centre of the room, upon which are also placed, the Constitution open ready for reading, a Bible, a knife and pens. Around the table the members shall stand in the order of office, except the initiator, who shall take his place in the line at the proper time. This line shall begin on the left hand side of the table, headed by the President. The members shall be dressed in black gowns and masks. The chief initiator shall be concealed in some portion of the room, in whatever manner the construction of the room and circumstances will permit. From this concealment he shall direct the ritual of initiation, coming forth only at the time of swearing eternal friendship and the giving of the hand-grasp of the Fraternity, to take his place in the line of members surrounding the table, returning immediately after to complete the ritual. Each initiate shall be led blindfolded into the Chamber of Mysteries, by the Warden, who shall then remove the bandage from his eyes. The initiator shall then say, 'Advance to the table before you. Place your right hand on the Bible you will find there.' When the initiate has done this the initiator shall say: 'This solemn oath, which you now take before the eyes and in the hearing of these your future brethren of the Fraternity of Book and Bond, is to be taken by you in the understanding of all that it purports and with the full intention that it shall be kept by you, clean, spotless and inviolate as long as life shall last. Repeat after me the following oath. I do solemnly swear to keep the secret from the world all things that shall transpire tonight within these walls.' After the initiate has repeated this the initiator shall say, 'you will advance to each figure in turn, giving each your left hand, and repeating to each 'I promise to be a true friend to you forever.' At this time the members, whom grasping the hand of the initiate shall give him the hand grasp and respond to his promise in the words, 'and I to you.' During the above mentioned rite the initiator shall take his place in the line of members surrounding the table returning to concealment immediately after he has shaken hands with the initiate. When the initiate has finished this rite the initiator shall say, 'return again to the table. On the table before you, lies the Constitution of the Fraternity of Book and Bond. Read it aloud.' When the initiate has finished the reading of the Constitution, the initiator shall say, 'turn again to the oath. Read it, and when you have finished say I _____ solemnly swear these things.' When the initiate has done this, the initiator shall say, 'turn to the end of the Constitution. On the table you will find a knife. Take it and cut the tip of the little finger of your left hand and sign the Constitution in your blood. (1903 Papers, Records of Book and Bond)

Initiation rituals were discontinued sometime between 1904 and 1911 and were replaced with initiation banquets, which provided a more festive civilized atmosphere.

Growth in the fraternity fluctuated over its history, but at least through the first decade, growth went from a handful of members to around forty at its peak. A note in the fraternity bulletin stated, *"...this is a gradual increase in the number of the fraternity. So far the increase has proven a benefit both from an internal and external point of view. Internally, the cohesion of the members has not suffered. The men 'hang together' in the old fashioned way making the Fraternity life a reality."* (April 1907 Fraternity Bulletin, Records of Book and Bond) As with all fraternities, each year's graduation took its toll on the fraternity memberships and during the early teens the fraternity found itself scrambling to increase memberships. By the end of 1915, only twelve active members remained.

Social events were common in the Fraternity of Book and Bond with members presenting numerous plays. Every year, two main events dominated the social life of the society. They were the annual banquet and annual dance, usually held in the spring. The annual banquet consisted of toasting, fraternity songs, and a five-course menu, followed by a relaxing social hour with cigars and cigarettes. The annual dance, an event that received a lot of attention from fraternity members, was typically held at an off campus location where numerous waltz and two-step dances passed the night. In 1914 the annual dance was held at the Lawn Club on May 2nd where forty couples, classily dressed, attended. Dancing promptly ended at midnight, and afterwards *"...refreshments were served, a number of those present joined in singing in a few of the good old songs, and as a most fit ending the fellows formed a ring and sang the Book and Bond song."* (1914 Bulletin, Records of Book and Bond)

BOOK AND BOND SONG

"Once again we meet, we men of Book and Bond;
Once again we meet in friendship true and strong;
Once again we meet, a jolly hearted throng;
We men of Book and Bond

CHORUS
Book and Bond we'll never sever,
Book and Bond we'll sing forever,

Book and Bond we'll sever never,
As long as life shall last

Here we pass the time in jollity and song;
Here we celebrate the pleasures of our Bond;
Here together thus the hours are never long,
In jolly Book and Bond

We'll sing again to-night of mystic Book and Bond;
We'll sing together of Phi Kappa Epsilon;
We'll sing her praises till the morning light shall dawn,
In mystic Book and Bond"

(1903 Annual Banquet Program, Records of Book and Bond)

In addition to fraternal social events, the members, in 1914, commissioned the Van Briggle Pottery to design and produce a fraternity mug based on the organization's symbol. The pottery was able to duplicate the design, in high relief, of a book wrapped with a belt engraved with the Phi Kappa Epsilon letters and the words "Book and Bond" written below. The mugs were a beautiful medium blue curdled glaze and marked 1914 on the bottom. Again, membership varied throughout the year of 1914, but records indicate that there were twenty-nine members throughout the 1914 school year. Records also indicate that the mug was most likely an item either given to the active members or a fraternal keepsake they could purchase as part of a mass order from the pottery. The exact number of mugs produced is unknown but it is safe to assume there were not many based solely on the membership numbers of the fraternity.

According to the Archives Department at the Yale Library between 1914-1917, seven students listed their hometown as Colorado Springs. It is unknown whether any of the students had influence over the Book and Bond mugs origination. However, at least two of the students were closely connected to the Van Briggle Pottery. Washington Pastorius, a member of the 1915 Yale graduating class, was the son of Horace & Elizabeth Pastorius of Colorado Springs, CO. Horace was the brother of C. Sharpless Pastorius who, a few years earlier, had been the treasurer of the pottery. The second direct tie to the pottery was with a student by the name of Ferguson Reddie Ormes. Ormes, the son of Manly D. and Jane Ormes, attended Yale one year to get a graduate degree in German from the college. His father, Manly D. Ormes, had graduated from Yale and wanted his son to do the same, but a lack of funds precluded him from attending for his undergraduate degree. *"My father (Manly Dayton Ormes, '85-B.D. '89) wanted me to go to Yale all the way, but we could not afford it. So I went for a repeat senior year...for graduate work in German."* (Forty-Five Year Record, Class of 1913, Yale College, pg. 186-187) The father, Manly D. Ormes, was not only the librarian at Colorado College, but an early pottery supporter, and the clergyman who officiated at the 1902 wedding of Artus and Anne Van Briggle. The exact ties may never be known as to why the Van Briggle Pottery was picked to create a specialty mug for the secretive Yale fraternity, but it is clear that there were definitely connections between the two distant groups— the Van Briggle Pottery in Colorado and Yale University in Connecticut.

Following a membership crisis of the mid-teens, the numbers began to grow steadily and the organization also became less secretive. Fraternity officers and events were made public in newspaper articles and through the representation of fraternity members in the Yale Inter-University Fraternity Council. Book and Bond officers realized a void in the fraternity's history existed, primarily due to secrecy, and therefore sent out letters to every known living former fraternity brother asking them to send in any historical data pertaining to the fraternity. While many items were thus re-created from memory or sent in from private collections, much of the history of the society was lost due to its secrecy. During the Great Depression, in 1935, the fraternity closed its doors and dissolved into a little-known piece of history associated with Yale University.

PHI KAPPA EPSILON SONG

"Midst pains and joys of college life
We sing fore'er of Book and Bond;
While others strive in painful strife,
We'll never quarrel in Book and Bond.

CHORUS

O Book and Bond, O Book and Bond,
In Thee we're locked in friendship fond:
The mystic Book will never fail;
The Bond is formed in love for Yale.

We'll sing to thee of friendship fair,
We'll drive old Sorrow from his lair;
The hours shall resound with glee,
Which every week we pass in thee.

When out upon life's sea we're cast,
Let him who lives to be the last
Of these good friends in mystic Bond
To this refrain with joy respond."

(1903 Annual Banquet Program, Records of Book and Bond)

Chapter 11

Odds and Ends

Many of the Van Briggle Pottery items already addressed in this book have a great amount of information available on their subjects. There are, however, many items scattered throughout the United States for which there is no information available. Some of these pieces are one-of-a kind, some were made in very small quantities, and some were even given away as promotional items.

It appears that the Van Briggle Pottery produced specialty pieces for two general periods: From 1907 to the early 1930s and from the 1960s to the present with the peak of specialty item production occurring in 1914. Catalogs well into the 1930s and 1940s mention the pottery as producers of *novelty items, wall plaques, and fountains.* The pieces discussed in this chapter show examples from both of the high production periods.

Obviously the Van Briggle Pottery wasn't the only common denominator linking all the subjects discussed in the book. Countless hours of scanning records, city directories, newspaper articles and books revealed that the Colorado Springs community was very closely knit. Examples such as Horace G. Lunt, a Colorado

District Judge, who was also a member of the Colorado Springs Park Commission and the administrator. He oversaw maintenance and upgrades to many of the city properties, one being the land on which the Bruin Inn was located. Additionally, Lunt was one of the men who bought the Van Briggle Pottery at a sheriff's auction in 1913 after the bankruptcy, and was elected president of the El Paso Club in 1898. Another being Charles B. Lansing, the staunch businessman, who also was a prominent member of the El Paso Club. He, too, was an owner of the Van Briggle Pottery and, during his tenure, as president of the company, the Reserve Watch plaques were made. Finally, one person who was the nucleus in the association between the pottery and the city was General William J. Palmer. Aside from founding the city, he was instrumental in the organization and early support of the pottery, he donated the land for the memorial pottery near monument creek, he was one of the principal stockholders of the pottery, he founded Colorado College and was its primary monetary supporter, he bought the land in North Cheyenne Cañon and renovated the Hatch cabin to become the Bruin Inn, and he was one of the first members of the original El Paso County Club. Through his life in Colorado Springs and up until his death, on March 13th, 1909, he made a tremendous impact in the development and shaping of the city. Palmer *"…believed that, when serving his or her own interests, the individual would create wealth that would benefit his or her fellow men & women."* (Loevy 12)

There is no doubt that the Van Briggle Pottery gave to the community both artistic value and name recognition. Either directly or indirectly, the pottery in some form influenced the lives and altered the paths of people in the community throughout the years. To what extent we may never know because no records of items or their production years exist. The history of the Van Briggle Pottery is, however, an integral part of the history of Colorado Springs and the United States.

Miscellaneous Specialty Items

World's Fair Paperweight – During the 1933 Chicago World's Fair, the pottery produced paperweights, similar to those made for the Colorado College fraternities, modeled after the 1933 World's Fair logo. It is not known if the items were sold at the fair or just made to commemorate the event.

Big Tree Convention Log Cabin – A commemorative smoker was produced by the Van Briggle Pottery for the Big Tree Convention, which was held in June 1926 in Colorado Springs.

Kissing Camels Golf Club – In the 1970s, the Kissing Camels Golf Club commissioned the Van Briggle Pottery to design and produce a commemorative desk ornament to celebrate the two hundredth club member.

Colorado Springs World Arena Tiles – The city of Colorado Springs built a facility in 1998 to house a variety of sporting and concert events; naming it the World Arena. Prior to it's opening, the city teamed up with the Van Briggle Pottery as a way to generate revenue to build the arena. The partnership allowed the Van Briggle Pottery to market four custom-made tile designs with donators' names engraved into the tiles. The tiles would then be permanently mounted in the World Arena throughout the halls. Donors could also purchase a duplicate tile as a keepsake.

"BRK" Mug – Little is known about this mug other than it was produced in the 1907 – 1912 period. It closely resembles CC fraternity mugs that were produced during the same period so there is the possibility that it was a personalized fraternity mug.

Antler's Garage Façade – The old Antlers Hotel, torn down in 1963, had an automotive garage located on the present day parking lot for the Pikes Peak Library in downtown Colorado Springs. When the garage was torn down in 1996, the city managed to preserve the façade and it stands today as the entrance into the library parking lot. The façade was a special production made with Van Briggle polychrome tiles for the Antlers Hotel. The garage was built in the spring of 1922 and promptly opened on June 1st 1922.

SAME Mug - The Society of American Military Engineers (SAME) is an organization designed to promote and facilitate engineering support for national security. This particular mug was made in the 1970s for the local Pikes Peak chapter.

NRA Plaque – This plaque was made for the NRA (National Recovery Administration). The eagle is a thunderbird, with one claw holding a gear and the other, bolts of electricity. The eagle symbol was usually blue and known as "the blue eagle." The Roosevelt administration created the NRA under the National Industrial Recovery Act, June 16, 1933. All major industries and even small businesses were supposed to develop and conform to standardized codes for production, prices, and employment practices. A business would receive a "Blue Eagle" symbol to tell the consumers that it was participating. Conservatives were opposed to interference with business, so the NRA died in mid-1935, when the Supreme Court determined that it gave too much legislative-type power directly to the president.

KSPZ Mug – KSPZ 92.9 is a longtime Colorado Springs radio station. In the 1970s, the station had the Van Briggle Pottery design and produce mugs. It is not known if the mugs were promotional items or for station employees.

Shriners' Hat – In the 1960s, the Shriners, possibly the local Colorado Springs chapter, had miniature Shriners hats produced in the Persian Rose glaze. It is not known if the items were given as gifts celebrating a special occasion or as awards to club members.

Lions Club Vase – This vase was produced in 1963 for a Colorado Lions Club event, either as a membership gift or award. The Lions Club is a service club dedicated to improving the lives of people in their communities through charitable activities.

Antlers Stag Mug – According to Craig Stevenson, the Antlers Hotel commissioned the Van Briggle Pottery to design a mug for the hotel, in the 1970s. The pottery came up with a simple design depicting a stags head glazed in a medium brown known as Russet.

Fort Vancouver Log Cabin – Fort Vancouver was the early establishment of the city of Vancouver, Washington. The settlement was first founded in 1825 by the Hudson Bay Company and headed by Dr. John McLoughlin who was put in charge of overseeing 700,000 acres of land. The settlement was the hub of all fur trading in the Pacific Northwest from 1828 until 1849 and it eventually closed in June of 1860. In 1925 two known items were produced to celebrate the one hundredth anniversary of the fort's founding – a commemorative Half Dollar and a Van Briggle Pottery Log Cabin smoker. Today the National Park Service owns and preserves the property.

Piccadilly Bar – Again, according to Craig Stevenson, the Antlers Hotel had a bar located inside known as the Piccadilly Bar. Some time in the late 1970s the bar commissioned several hundred mugs as promotional items to accompany a special drink when ordered. The mugs came in three known glazes, high gloss orange/brown, high gloss mocha brown, and high gloss cream. The mug was originally designed by Craig Stevenson.

World's Fair Vase – During the 1933 Chicago World's Fair, the pottery modified an existing Van Briggle vase to resemble tree bark and marked it with World's Fair 1933. It is not known if the items were sold at the fair or just made to commemorate the event.

Colorado Springs Association of Life Underwriters Bookends – Colorado Springs Association of Life Underwriters is a coop of independent life insurance representatives. This set of bookends, depicting Pikes Peak was presented to Sam Baum on December 12th 1974.

American Numismatics Association – The American Numismatic Association, located in Colorado Springs, is an organization that encourages and educates people to collect and study money related items. This mug was produced by the pottery as a promotional item in the 1970s.

Broadmoor Hotel Ashtray – The Broadmoor Hotel began its origins in 1891 as a gambling casino. Later Colorado Springs dignitaries Winfield Scott Stratton and Spencer Penrose both took turns owning and running the hotel. Today the hotel is a five star and diamond hotel and hosts prominent guests visiting the Pikes Peak region.

The Van Briggle ashtray produced in the 1970s shows a depiction of polo players at the top, which possibly gives away its origins.

"MLL" Mug – Little is known about this mug other than it was produced in the 1907 – 1912 period. It closely resembles CC fraternity mugs that were produced during the same period so there is the possibility that it was a personalized fraternity mug.

California State Employees Association Chalice – CSEA is California's largest state employee organization, representing state and university workers, managers, supervisors and retirees before the California Legislature and key state departments and agencies. It is not known why this item was produced.

Radio Cases – After the Lewis brothers purchased the Van Briggle Pottery they attempted to expand the business while cutting costs. One such measure was to expand the business into previously untouched areas of the commercial market. They built custom high frequency ceramic radio cases. The radio cases were primarily marketed to specialized businesses such as the Pinkerton National Detective Agency for remote communications. Complete radio systems had a suggested retail of $79.00

Marksheffel Garage Building – *"The Marksheffel Garage at Colorado Springs is the largest and most modern garage in the world. It has a frontage of 312 feet and a depth of 195 feet, and covers 46,000 square feet all on the ground floor, and has a basement under the whole building."* (Higbee News, Howard County, MO, 1917) The business boasted a beautifully furnished ladies bathroom with all modern conveniences. It also housed a billiard room and cigar store for the men. The Marksheffel Garage had a clock mounted on the top façade of the building. Surrounding the clock was Van Briggle polychrome terra cotta edging and words depicting *"Love Makes Time Go Time Makes Love Go".* There were also two large polychrome Cadillacs on each side, adjacent to the clock. The garage was torn down in 1966 and was on the site of the current Penrose Library.

Masonic Temple Plaque – In 1908 the Colorado Springs Masonic Temple commissioned the Van Briggle Pottery to design a helping hands or brotherhood plaque depicting a pair of hands shaking. Currently the plaque's whereabouts are unknown.

Glencora Kindig Memorial Plaque – Glendora Kindig was an extremely popular teacher in the early 1900s. She taught at the old Steele Elementary School that was located at 1720 N. Weber St. Following her sudden death in October 1908, Reverend J. H. Franklin hired the pottery to design and build a memorial plaque in her honor. The plaque was designed by Mae E. Cook and was 3' x 4' in size. The plaque design was of trees in the background and a woman standing in the center. The woman in the plaque was representative of education. Additionally, a small silver plate carried a memorial inscription. The plaque was installed in the main hall of the school around Easter of 1909. During a renovation project in the summer of 1950, the plaque was accidentally destroyed.

This Page Intentionally Left Blank

Color Plates

Compilation Photos by

David O. Swint Jr.

1914 Bruin Inn Mug
(Author's Collection)

1908 Colorado College
Barbecue Tumbler
(Author's Collection)

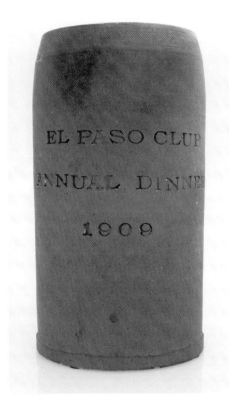

1909 El Paso Club Mug
(Author's Collection)

1914 Heidelberg Inn Mug
(Author's Collection)

L to R Top Row: 1914 Half Way House/Sigma Chi Mug, 1907 - 1912 Kappa Sigma Mug, 1907 - 1912 Phi Gamma Delta Mug
L to R Bottom Row: 1907 - 1912 Kappa Sigma Mug, 1916 Phi Gamma Delta Mug
(Author's Collection)

1922 Kappa Sigma Smoker
(Todd Sutherland Collection)

1920/30s Sigma Chi Paperweight
(Collection of Bob Teas &
Kathy Honea)

1907 - 1912 Phi Gamma Delta Mug
(Photo Courtesy of Colorado Springs Pioneers
Museum Starsmore Center for Local History
Colorado Springs, CO USA)

1920/30s Kappa Sigma Paperweight
(Author's Collection)

1914 Colorado College
Sigma Chi/Half Way House Mug
(Author's Collection)

1914 Mission Inn Chamberstick
(Photo Courtesy of Rago Arts & Auction
Center/Lambertville NJ)

1914 Mission Inn Tumbler
(Photo Courtesy of the Van Briggle Pottery)

1914 Mission Inn Pitcher
(Photo Courtesy of Richard Sasicki)

1919 Reserve Watch Plaque
(Author's Collection)

1914 Yale University Fraternity
of Book and Bond Mug
(Author's Collection)

1933 Worlds Fair Paperweight
(Private Collection)

1926 Big Tree Club Convention Smoker
(Miles Schmidt Collection)

1970s Kissing Camel Golf Club
Commemorative Item
(Van Briggle Pottery Collection)

1990s Colorado Springs World
Arena Decorative Tile
(Author's Collection)

1907 - 1912 Personalized Mug
(Author's Collection)

1922 Antlers Hotel Garage Facade
(Currently at the Entrance to the
Penrose Public Library Parking Lot)

1970s Unknown Mug
(Author's Collection)

1970s Personalized Tumbler
(Author's Collection)

1970s Society of American Military Engineers (SAME) Mug
(Author's Collection)

1930s NRA Plaque
(Photo Courtesy of the Van Briggle Pottery)

1970s **KSPZ (Z93) Coffee Mug**
(Author's Collection)

1960s Miniature Shriners Hat
(Miles Schmidt Collection)

1963 Colorado Lions Club Commemorative Vase
(Miles Schmidt Collection)

1970s Antlers Hotel Mug
(Van Briggle Pottery Collection)

1925 Fort Vancouver Smoker
(Miles Schmidt Collection)

1970s Antlers Hotel Piccadilly Bar Mug
(Author's Collection)

1933 World's Fair Vase
(Miles Schmidt Collection)

1933 World's Fair Vase
(Miles Schmidt Collection)

1970s Antlers Hotel Piccadilly Bar Mug
(Photo Courtesy of Colorado Springs Pioneers
Museum Starsmore Center for Local History
Colorado Springs, CO USA)

1974 Colorado Springs Association of Life Underwriters
(Private Collection)

1970s American Numismatics Association Mug
(Author's Collection)

1970s Broadmoor Hotel Ashtray
(Private Collection)

1907 - 1912 Personalized Mug
(Author's Collection)

1980 California State Employees
Association Chalice
(Private Collection)

1920s Van Briggle Pottery Flier
outlining the features of custom high
frequency (HF) radios
(Courtesy of the Van Briggle Pottery)

MODEL B. LONG DISTANCE RADIO RECEIVER.

CABINET: Genuine Van Briggle vetrified cabinet, manufactured by the World Famous Van Briggle Pottery of the best heat-resisting insulating materials obtainable. The cabinet is made in one piece and fired to a temperature of 2500 degrees Fahrenheit. At this high temperature the materials fuse, forming a compact vetrified insulated cabinet that eliminates body capacity effects. The cabinet is finished in the turquoise blue, which has made the Van Briggle ware world famous, making the radio set an ornament suitable for any home.

PANEL: Formica 3-16 inch thick, Gorton Engraved and filled in with Brilliant White. All connections and readings plainly indicated. Size, 7x9 inches.

KNOBS: Adjustable, tapered and finely fluted for greatest ease in manipulation.

BINDING POSTS: Lock nut type insuring positive connection.

RHEOSTAT: Half-revolution type smooth running and non-heating.

INDUCTANCE: Cylindrical Windings on Formica Tubing correctly proportioned to give minimum capacity and perfect control of regeneration.

SOCKET: Metal-Shell construction on Formica base to fit Standard Tubes.

FIXED CAPACITY: Of approved Mica and Copper construction reducing diaelectric losses.

ROTATING PARTS: Steel Shafts running in long single brass bearings, resulting in smooth operation and perfect alignment.

WIRING: Of flexible Copper Cable protected by Varnished Tubing, resulting in flexibility and avoiding any possibility of broken connections. Moving contacts in tuning circuit fully pigtailed, eliminating all "noise."

METAL PARTS: With exception of rotating shafts, brass, Satin nickel plated.

CIRCUIT: Fundamental Armstrong Regenerative, so designed and applied as to eliminate all "dead ending" losses combined with very fine selectivity in tuning.

AMPLIFICATION: Two steps of Audio Frequency amplification may be obtained when desired, mounted in a like cabinet to match the detector unit.

DISTANCE: Under favorable atmospheric conditions the range is 1000 to 1500 miles.

GUARANTEE: We guarantee results when installed and operated according to our plain and simple printed instructions. If you are not entirely satisfied, return the instrument and your money will be cheerfully refunded.

Van Briggle Tile & Pottery Co.,
COLORADO SPRINGS, COLORADO

1914 - 1966 The Marksheffel Garage Facade
(Courtesy Pikes Peak Library District &
Stewarts Commercial Photographers)

Price Guide

1914 Bruin Inn Mug (Pg. 129) .... $600 - $700

1908 CC Barbecue Tumbler (Pg. 130) .... $600 - $700

1909 El Paso Club Mug (Pg. 131) .... $400 - $500

1914 Heidelberg Inn Mug (Pg. 132) .... $800 - $900

CC Fraternity Mugs (Pg. 133)
L to R Top Row:
    1914 Sigma Chi Mug .... $1500 - $1600
    1907-1912 Kappa Sigma Mug .... $500 - $600
    1907-1912 Phi Gamma Delta Mug .... $900 - $1000
L to R Bottom Row:
    1907-1912 Kappa Sigma Mug .... $500 - $600
    1916 Phi Gamma Delta Mug .... $600 - $700

CC Fraternity Items (Pg. 134)
L to R Top Row:
    1922 Kappa Sigma Smoker .... $400 - $500
L to R Bottom Row:
    1920/30s Sigma Chi Paperweight .... $200 - $300
    1907-1912 Phi Gamma Delta Mug .... $600 - $700
    1920/30s Kappa Sigma Paperweight .... $200 - $300

1914 Sigma Chi/Half Way House Mug (Pg. 135)............................$1500 - $1600

1914 Mission Inn Chamberstick (Pg. 136)................................$1300 - $1400

1914 Mission Inn Tumbler (Pg. 136).....................................$1000 - $1100

1914 Mission Inn Pitcher (Pg. 136).....................................$1300 - $1400

1919 Reserve Watch Plaque (Pg. 137)....................................$900 - $1000

1914 Book and Bond Mug (Pg. 138).......................................$1500 - $1600

Miscellaneous (Pg. 139)
L to R Top Row:
    1933 Worlds Fair Paperweight ....$250 - $350
    1926 Big Tree Club Convention Smoker..............................$400 - $500
L to R Bottom Row:
    1970s Kissing Camels Golf Club Commemorative Item.........$150 - $250
    1990s World Arena Decorative Tile ....$40 - $50
    1907 – 1912 Personalized Mug......................................$350 - $450

Miscellaneous (Pg. 140)
L to R Top Row:
    1970s Unknown Mug...$25 - $40
    1970s Personalized Tumbler ....$20 - $30
L to R Bottom Row:
    1970s Society of American Military Engineers Mug.................$25 - $40
    1930s NRA Plaque...$300 - $400

Miscellaneous (Pg. 141)
L to R Top Row:
 1970s KSPZ Z93 Mug .... $25 - $35
 1960s Miniature Shriners Hat.. $100 - $150
L to R Bottom Row:
 1963 Colorado Lions Club Commemorative Vase .... $60 - $70
 1970s Antlers Hotel Stag Mug .... $75 - $100

Miscellaneous (Pg. 142)
L to R Top Row:
 1925 Fort Vancouver Smoker... $25 - $35
 1970s Piccadilly Bar Mug .... $40 - $50
L to R Bottom Row:
 1933 World's Fair Vase .... $90 - $100
 1970s Piccadilly Bar Mug... $40 - $50

Miscellaneous (Pg. 143)
L to R Top Row:
 1974 Pikes Peak Bookends .... $25 - $35
 1970s ANA Mug .... $40 - $50
L to R Bottom Row:
 1970s Broadmoor Hotel Ashtray .... $125 - $150
 1907 – 1912 Personalized Mug.. $350 - $450
 1980 CSEA Chalice .... $75 - $100

Works Cited

"1903 Bruin Inn Renovation Plans." Map. Special Collections, Tutt Library, Colorado College, Colorado Springs, Colorado. vertical files.

1906 Bruin Inn Renovation Plans. Special Collections, Tutt Library, Colorado College, Colorado Springs, Colorado. vertical files.

1916 Bruin Inn Renovation Plans. Special Collections, Tutt Library, Colorado College, Colorado Springs, Colorado. vertical files.

Abbott, Morris W. The Rise and Fall of the Half Way House. Vol. 24. Boulder, Colorado : Johnson Company, 1968. 192-210. The Denver Westerners Brand Book.

Arnest, Mark. "The Legacy of Artus Van Briggle." Colorado Springs Gazette 12 Dec. 1999: 7, col. 4.

Bogue, Dorothy M. The Van Briggle Story. 2nd ed. Colorado Springs, Colorado: Century One Press, 1976.

"Bruin Inn Advertising Pamphlet." Colorado Springs, Colorado, 1940.

"Bruin Inn Renovation Plans." 1903. Special Collections, Tutt Library, Colorado College, Colorado Springs, Colorado.

"Bruin Inn Renovation Plans." 1906. Special Collections, Tutt Library, Colorado College, Colorado Springs, Colorado.

"Bruin Inn Renovation Plans." 1916. Special Collections, Tutt Library, Colorado College, Colorado Springs, Colorado.

Coffman, Edward M. "World War I." <u>World Book, Inc.</u>. 18 June 2004
        <http://www.aolsvc.worldbook.aol.com>. World Book Online Reference Center, 2004

Colorado City Iris 21 Nov. 1913.

Colorado City Iris 6 Jan. 1916.

"Colorado College Song Book." Colorado Springs, Colorado: Colorado College, 1910.

"Colorado College Song Book." Colorado Springs, Colorado: Colorado College, 1918.

Colorado College Tiger Newspaper 20 Dec. 1907: 14, col 2.

Colorado College Tiger Newspaper 9 Oct. 1908: 1,col. 3.

Colorado College Tiger Newspaper 9 Oct. 1908: 2, col. 1.

Colorado College Tiger Newspaper 24 Oct. 1908: 11.

Colorado College Tiger Newspaper 30 Oct. 1908: 1, col. 2.

Colorado College Tiger Newspaper 6 Nov. 1908: 1, col. 1.

Colorado College Tiger Newspaper 6 Nov. 1908: 1, col. 2.

Colorado College Tiger Newspaper 6 Nov. 1908: 3, col. 2.

Colorado College Tiger Newspaper 19 Feb. 1909: 14, col. 2.

Colorado College Tiger Newspaper 1 Oct. 1909: 11, col. 1

Colorado College Tiger Newspaper 5 Nov. 1909: 13, col. 2-3.

Colorado College Tiger Newspaper 27 Apr. 1915: 3, col. 4.

Colorado Springs Gazette 25 Aug. 1901: 10

Colorado Springs Gazette 7 Dec. 1901: 5 col. 1-2

Colorado Springs Gazette 1 Jan. 1904: 15 col. 2

Colorado Springs Gazette 3 Dec. 1908: 7, col. 1-7.

Colorado Springs Gazette 26 Oct. 1913: 7 col. 6-7

Colorado Springs Gazette 30 Oct. 1914: 8, col. 1.

Colorado Springs Gazette 2 July 1917: 5, col. 2.

Colorado Springs Gazette 4 July 1917: 5, col. 2.

Colorado Springs Gazette 13 Dec. 1917: 4, col. 1.

Colorado Springs Gazette 14 Sept. 1919: 7, col. 2.

Colorado Springs Gazette 10 Apr. 1920: 1 col. 3

Colorado Springs Gazette Telegraph 19 Dec. 1954, sec. B: 1, col. 1-2.

Colorado Springs Gazette Telegraph 10 May 1956: 2 col. 5-7

Colorado Springs Gazette 12 Dec. 1999: 7, col.4.

Curtis, Edmund D., <u>Pottery Its Craftsmanship And Its Appreciation</u>. New York and London: Harper & Brothers Publishers., 1940.

Cutler Hall. 1870. Special Collections, Tutt Library, Colorado College, Colorado Springs, Colorado. vertical files

Evans, Paul. "California's Mission Inn." <u>The Spinning Wheel</u> Nov. 1976: 32-33.

Fort Vancouver National Historic Site . National Park Service. 18 June 2004 <http://www.nps.gov/fova/home.htm>.

"Van Briggle Adds to Colorado's Fame." Glass and Pottery World, No. 4 Apr. 1908: 15-16

Higbee News 1917, Howard County, Missouri

"Information Paper." Colorado Springs, Colorado: Van Briggle Pottery Company, July, 1972.

James Kerr House. 1890. Special Collections, Tutt Library, Colorado College, Colorado Springs, Colorado. vertical files.

Klotz, Esther., Curl Alan. <u>The Mission Inn: Its History and Artifacts</u>. Corona, CA: UBS Printing Group., 1993.

Loevy, Robert D. <u>Colorado College: A Place of Learning 1874-1999</u>. Colorado Springs, Colorado: Colorado College, 1999. 12.

Long Distance Radio Receiver Advertisement. 18 June 2004, c. 1920, Van Briggle Pottery.

Nelson, Scott H., Lois K. Crouch, Euphemia B. Demmin, and Robert Wyman Newton. <u>A Collectors Guide to Van Briggle Pottery</u>. Indiana, PA: A. G. Halldin Publishing Co., Inc., 1986.

Ormes, Ferguson R. "Forty-Five Year Record, Class of 1913, Yale College." 1958. Edited by Sidney Lovett, published with the assistance of the Class Officers Bureau.

Petition to Incorporate the Township of Ramona. El Paso County 1913.

"Ramona City Town Plot." Map. Colorado Springs, Colorado, USA: Colorado Springs Pioneer Museum, Starsmore Center for Local History, 1913.

"Records of Book and Bond." 1903, Annual Banquet Program, Yale University (RU60), Manuscripts and Archives, Yale University Library.

"Records of Book and Bond." 1903,Fraternity Bulletin, Yale University (RU60), Manuscripts and Archives, Yale University Library.

"Records of Book and Bond." April, 1907, fraternity bulletin, Yale University (RU60), Manuscripts and Archives, Yale University Library

"Records of Book and Bond." 1911, Initiation Banquet Program, Yale University (RU60), Manuscripts and Archives, Yale University Library.

"Records of Book and Bond." 1914, fraternity bulletin, Yale University (RU60), Manuscripts and Archives, Yale University Library.

Rudd, C. E. "Records of Book and Bond." 1908, Yale University, (RU 60), Manuscripts and Archives, Yale University Library.

Sargent, Irene. "Chinese Pots and Modern Faience." The Craftsman, VI, No. IV. Sept. 1903

Seibel, Harriett. A History of the Colorado Springs Schools District 11, Colorado Springs, CO: century one press, 1975. 66-67.

Shinn, Alice. Letter to The Broadmoor Art Academy. 1929. Colorado Springs Pioneer Museum, Colorado Springs, Colorado.

Sprague, Marshall. Newport In the Rockies. 4th ed. Athens, Ohio: Swallow P, 1987. 212.

Stevenson, Craig Owner-Manager, Van Briggle Art Pottery Company, Colorado Springs, CO Personal interview. 16 June 2004.

The Mission Inn Museum. The Mission Inn Hotel, 3696 Main Street, Riverside, California 92501. 20 June 2004 <http://www.missioninnmuseum.com>.

The Pikes Peak Nugget. Vol. VIII. Denver Colorado: The Great Western Publishing Company, 1907.

The Pikes Peak Nugget. Vol. IX. Colorado Springs: The Prompt Printery, 1908. 180.

"The Van Briggle Connection." Flash Point-The Quarterly Bulletin of the Tile Heritage Foundation (April-June, 1992).

"Van Briggle Advertising Pamphlets." Colorado Springs, Colorado, 1907 – 1960s.

Van Briggle, Artus. Letter to Frank Riddle. 2 Mar. 1904.

"Van Briggle Pottery." Colorado Springs, Colorado: Van Briggle Pottery, 1907, advertising catalogue.

"Van Briggle Pottery." Colorado Springs, Colorado: Van Briggle Pottery, 1912, advertising catalogue.

"Van Briggle Pottery." Colorado Springs, Colorado: Van Briggle Pottery, 1914. advertising catalogue.

Van Briggle Pottery: The Early Years. Colorado Springs Fine Arts Center, Colorado Springs, CO, 1975. (Barbara M. Arnest, Editor; Robert E. Morris, Editorial Associate; Robert Wyman Newton, The Catalogue; Lois K. Corush and Euphemia B. Demmin, Research Associates.)

Index

ABETT, MRS., 13
ACADEMIE JULIAN, 7
AHLERS, MRS., 13
ALLEN, MRS., 13
AMERICAN SEWER PIPE COMPANY, 22
ARTHUR, CHESTER, A. MR AND MRS.,
  13
ARTS AND CRAFTS SOCIETY OF
  BOSTON, 19
AVON POTTERY, 7

BANGS, HARRY, 11, 18
BARTOW, MRS., 13
BEAUX ARTS, 7
BETA OMEGA, 76
BEMIS, MISS, 13
BIG TOOTH RESERVOIR, 92
BOAS, MRS., 13
BOOK AND BOND, 3, 107-110, 112-118,
  138, 147, 153
BOOTH, EDWARD, 84
          MANVILLE, 84
BROADMOOR HOTEL, 78, 124, 148
BROADMOOR ART ACADEMY, THE,
  153
BROWN, MRS., 13
BRUCE, O.F., 26
BRUIN INN, 2, 3, 32-44, 52, 90, 91, 120, 129,
  146
BRUIN INN NOVELTY ORCHESTRA, 41

BRYAN, MARTHA, 6
BUCKMAN, GEORGE REX, 13
BURGESS, W.N., 13
BURNETT, FRANK, 72

CHEYENNE CANON, 32, 36, 41, 120
          NORTH, 32, 36, 41, 120
          SOUTH, 32
CHI SIGMA, 76
CHISHOLM, R, 13
CINCINNATI ART SCHOOL, 6
CLARK, CHARLES, 56
COLORADO CITY, 66, 67, 68, 70, 71, 73,
  74, 149
COLORADO COLLEGE, 3, 5, 8, 22, 24, 28,
  32-36, 38-40, 45-54, 58, 76, 77, 80, 81, 90,
  91, 120, 121, 149-152
COLORADO COLLEGE LAND
  COMPANY, 32, 34
COLORAOD SPRINGS, 2, 5, 6, 8, 9, 14,
  16-29, 32, 34, 35, 36, 38, 40, 41, 46-48, 54,
  56-58, 61, 64, 66-72, 74, 77, 78, 91, 102-105,
  116, 119, 120-126, 139, 142, 143, 149-153
COLORADO SPRINGS CHAMBER OF
  COMMERCE, 24
COLORADO SPRINGS WORLD ARENA,
  29, 121, 139
CONNER, JAMES C., 13
CRAIG, CHARLES, 11, 13
CRIPPLE CREEK, 23, 27, 61

CROSBY, MISS, 13
CUB, THE, 40
CURTIS, EDMUND, 22, 23, 39, 97, 151

DICKMAN, FOSTER, MISS, 13
DIX, LYLE, 21
DODGE, CLARENCE P., 14
DONALDSON, D.V., MRS., 13
DORSEY, MRS., 13
DOTY, MIKE, 5, 80

ECCLESIA, 79
EHRICH, MRS. AND MISS, 13
EL PASO CLUB, 59-64, 131, 146
EL PASO COUNTY CLUB, 56, 60
EUSTIS, MR., 13

FISHER, T.J., 15
FRENCH A.T., 37, 50
FRENCH, BESSIE, 13

GALLOP, HOWARD, 14
GAMMA DELTA, 75, 76, 78, 79, 82, 133,
 134, 146
GAZETTE, 9, 14, 18, 20, 25, 47, 57, 58, 68,
 70, 103, 104, 149-151
GAZETTE TELEGRAPH, 27, 67, 70, 151
GEIGER, GEORGE, 67, 70-72
GOLD ORE GLAZE, 27
GRUEBY, 9
GUNN, FRANK, 89
       KATIE, 89, 90

HALF WAY HOUSE, 75, 80, 83, 86, 88-93,
 133, 135, 147, 149
HAMES, BYRON, 66
HAMP, SIDFORD F., 13
HATCH, WALTER M., 32
HAGERMAN, PERCY, 13
HARRIS, WILLIAM H., 90, 91
HAYDEN, DR., 13
HAYES, MRS., 13
HEIDELBERG INN, 65, 71-74, 132, 146
HIGMAN, WILLIAM, 26
HILLE, E.W., 37, 50
HOMESTEAD ACT, 84
HOPKINS, GENE, 26
HOWBERT, IRVING, 13
HULL, CLEM, 26

JACKSON, WM. S., 56
      HELEN HUNT, 34, 56

KAPPA SIGMA, 2, 39, 75-80, 82, 133, 134,
 146
KERR, JAMES H., 58, 152
KINKEAD, EMMA, 20, 39
KINSMAN, CLARENCE, 67, 70
KISSELL, MR. AND MRS., 14
KRAUSE, GEORGE, 23

LACEY, JIM, 66
LANSING, CHARLES B., 25, 29, 56, 120
LANGENBECK, KARL, 6
LAVLEY, J.E., 34, 36

LEWIS, I.F., 25, 27, 125
        J.H., 25, 28, 125
LEWIS AND CLARK EXPOSITION, 19
LILLY, JOSEPH F., 34, 36
LITTLE LONDON, 60
LOOMIS, MISS, 13
LOTAVE, MR., 13
LOUVRE, MUSEE DES ARTS,
  DECORATFIS, 7
LUNT, H.G., 23, 119
        MRS., 14

MAC NEILL, C.M., 15
MACLAREN, T., 13
MANITOU AND PIKES PEAK RAILWAY,
  86
MARTIN, ELIZABETH, 13
MCCLURG, MR AND MRS., 13
McREYNOLDS, JAMES, 67, 68
MIDLAND RAILROAD ROUND HOUSE,
  28
MING DYNASTY, 7
MOATS, LENNIE, 68, 71

NICHOLS, JOSEPHE DR, 13
NOBLE, CHARLES, E., 13
NOKOMIS LODGE, 88
NOYES, MR. AND MRS., 13

OHIO STATE UNIVERSITY, 18
O'NEAL, BILL, 72

PALSGROVE, THOMAS, 84, 89
        NETTIE, 86, 89
        JOHN B., 89
        JENNIE, 89, 90
PALMER, WILLIAM J., GENERAL, 14, 19,
  34, 36, 56, 59, 120
PARSONS, PROFESSOR, 14
PASTORIUS, C.SHARPLESS, 14, 15, 116
        ELIZABETH, 116
        FRANCIS, 13
        HORACE, 13, 116
        WASHINGTON, 116
PEAVEY, DR., 13
PERKINS, FLORENCE, 22
PERKINS, FRANK, 13
PHI DELTA THETA, 76, 80
PHI GAMMA DELTA, 75, 76, 78, 79, 82,
  133, 134, 146
PIKES PEAK COG RAILWAY, 84
PIKES PEAK TRAIL HOUSE, 86
PLATTE AVENUE, 58, 60, 64

RAMONA, 2, 66, 68-74, 152, 153
REED, JACOB, DR., 56
REMICK, MAJOR, 14
RICHARDS, WILLIAM A., 84, 86
RIDDLE, FRANK, 15-18, 21, 22, 154
RIDGEWAY, MISS AND MRS, 14
RILEY, KENNETH F., 36

RITTER, ETIENNE A., 21
        ANNE , 26

ROOKWOOD POTTERY, 6-9
RUXTON CREEK, 84, 88

SCHLEGEL, AMBROSE, 16, 21
SHETT, DR. AND MRS., 13
SHIELDS, JOHN, 14
SHINN, ALICE, 9-11, 15, 22, 26, 153
SIGMA CHI, 39, 75, 76, 80, 82, 83, 133-135, 146, 147
SIMPSON, JUDGE AND MRS., 13
SKELTON, MR. AND MRS., 13
SOLENBERGER, DR AND MRS., 13
SOLLY, DR. AND MRS., 13, 56
SOUTTER, MR. AND MRS., 13
ST. LOUIS LOUISIANA PURCHASE EXPOSITION, 17
STEVENSON, KEN, 28, 29
          CRAIG, 5, 28, 29, 124, 153
          BERTHA, 28
          JEFF, 28
STEPHENSON, E.P., 56
STEWART, PHILLIP B., 13
STORER, MARIA, 7-9, 11, 14
STRATTON, W.S., 15, 124
STRIEBY, WILLIAM, 8, 9, 13, 15, 46, 47
SUTTON, ASAHEAL, 8, 13, 15
          BILLY, 8
SWAN, MRS AND MISS, 14
SWANSON, LEE, 36

TAYLOR, MRS., 13
TENNEY, E.P., 32

TEJON STREET, 2, 8, 58, 59, 64
THOMAS, ALTON D., 13
THOMPSON, MRS., 13
THOMPSON, H.C., 67, 70
THORNDALE PARK, 74
TIGER, COLORADO COLLEGE, 36, 39, 49, 50, 52, 91, 150
TOWNSEND, S.W., 14
TUBERCULOSIS, 8, 11

VALENTINE, ALBERT, 8
VAN BRUEGHEL, 6
VAN BRIGGLE, 1-4, 17-20, 24, 27-29, 39, 47, 49, 50, 53, 61, 71, 78, 81, 116, 122, 124, 125, 144, 149, 152, 154
VAN BRIGGLE, ANNE, 7, 9, 10, 11, 14, 15, 18, 19-21, 25-27, 30, 116
          ARTUS, 6-12, 14-18, 25, 30, 46, 61, 116, 149, 154
          EUGENE, 6
VAN BRIGGLE POTTERY, 4, 6, 10-12, 22, 25, 27, 28, 30, 39, 46, 47, 56, 61, 63, 76, 78, 91, 97, 98, 104, 115-117, 119, 120, 121, 122, 123, 125, 126, 139-141, 144, 152, 153
VAN BRIGGLE SCHOOL OF DESIGN, 25, 26
VAN DEN AREND, NICHOLAS, 19, 20

WALKER, NELLIE, 26
WILLS, FRED, 26
WRIGHT, FRANK LLOYD, 20
WRIGHT-INGRAHMAN, ELIZABETH, 20

159 The Story Behind the Clay

WRIGHT, LILLY AND COMPANY, 34

YALE, 5, 107, 108, 116-118, 138, 153

The authors are always interested in purchasing examples
of Van Briggle specialty pieces and related items. Please send any correspondence to
vanbrigglebook@aol.com